A Devotional for Dads and Their Daughters

DAUGHTERS OF THE KING

DAUGHTERS OF THE KING
A Devotional for Dads and Their Daughters
2025 (c) by Freddie Prado
All rights reserved. Published 2025.

BIBLE SCRIPTURES

Published in the United States of America

Spirit Media and our logos are trademarks of Spirit Media

 **SPIRIT MEDIA**
www.spiritmedia.us

8045 Arco Corporate Dr STE 130
Raleigh, NC 27617
1 (888) 800-3744

Books > Religion & Spirituality > Christian Books & Bibles >
Christian Living > Family & Relationships
Paperback ISBN: 9798893071467
Library of Congress Control Number: 2025910018

"There once was a daughter, created in the image of the Father."

Contents

A Note to My Girls

To my girls, Caitie Bug, Aria girl, Jenna Jo, and Shiloh Ann: Papi loves you so much. When I became a dad, I never realized how fun and exciting it would be to be a girl dad. Each of you is a gift from God, and I want to share my heart with you. Papi is nowhere near perfect. I've made mistakes, and every day I have a chance to grow and become the man God has called me to be. But you have a Father in heaven who never messes up. You belong to Him, and I have the incredible honor of taking care of you and being your dad here on earth. For the rest of my life, I will do my best to teach you about our heavenly Father, who created you and has amazing plans for your lives.

You girls are strong, brave, hardworking, funny, beautiful, and you amaze me more every day. You each have so much of your momma in you—little superwomen. Caitie, you are full of grace, wisdom, and courage. You can beat any boy at sports, and hearing you sing is one of Papi's favorite sounds in the world. Always remember, you don't have to be perfect, and you were created to use your gifts to lead people into God's presence. Aria, you have the biggest heart, an incredible mind, and your imagination will make a big impact on this world. Never forget, your emotions are a gift, but they don't control you. Use your heart and your voice to teach people about God and show them His love through how you care for others. Jenna Jo, you are so funny, fashionable, and an amazing leader. You know exactly what you want, and you bring so much joy to everyone around you. People follow you because God made you a leader—so lead them towards Jesus. Shiloh Ann, you carry a light that only comes from the Holy Spirit. You're smart, and a little warrior. You might be Mommy and Papi's youngest daughter, But God made you to do great things for His kingdom. Keep learning from your sisters, and always know you carry the peace of Jesus wherever you go.

To all my Prado girls, remember this about God:

"If you look for me wholeheartedly, you will find me." (Jeremiah 29:13 NLT)

Spend your lives devoted to discovering who the Father created you to be, who Jesus is, and where the Holy Spirit is leading you.

One day at a time.
One step at a time.
One miracle at a time.
Papi loves you.

A Note to Your Girl(s)

Before beginning the daughters of the King journey with your daughter(s), take some time to write a note to them from your heart. Even if it takes a little while, use this moment to speak life into her identity and future. The words you share will have a big impact and will lay a foundation for her to walk on in life. Ask God what His heart is for your daughter and together let's lead our girls toward their Heavenly Father.

_____

_____

_____

_____

_____

_____

_____

_____

_____

_____

_____

_____

_____

_____

_____

_____

_____

Part One:

Who is God?

"In the beginning God created the heavens and the earth."
Genesis 1:1, NIV

Lesson 1:

Who Made It?

Have you ever eaten something really delicious? I'm not talking about just any type of snack. I'm talking about the kind of food that makes your mouth water, your stomach grumble, and has you sniffing around like a lion ready to find what you're looking for and pounce! Maybe it's some ooey, gooey, cheesy mac 'n' cheese made by your grandma? Or a street taco with all the heavenly toppings— don't forget the guac! Whether it's your favorite dish your mom makes or breakfast your dad whipped up on a Saturday morning, good food hits the spot!

Now, for just a minute, I want you to think about the person who made that wonderful food. How did they make it? Did they add a pinch of salt, a swig of sauce, or maybe a ton of butter? Did they bake it, sauté it, fry it, or flambé it? You see, the person who knows a dish best is the chef who created it. They know what it took to transform simple ingredients into a delicious meal that's good for the soul. No one knows a dish better than the chef who created it.

Now let's shift gears. Who made you? Who put the hairs on your head, the toes on your feet, and who gave you a belly button? What incredible creator could've put that amazing smile on your face and made you fast and strong enough to beat the boys in a race? The Bible says, "In the beginning, God..." Before anything came to be, there was God. He is the start of it all, and He started it all. Nobody created God, but the Bible says, "In the beginning, God created..." God was the main chef, and what did He make?

"In the beginning God created the heavens and the earth" (Genesis 1:1 NIV)

But His creation didn't stop there. He made light, trees, the birds, and the bees! God made oceans, beautiful flowers, and He even made tiny little ladybugs. If you think all that is cool, check this out! The Bible says, "So God created human beings in His own image. In the image of God, He created them; male and female, He created them." (Genesis 1:27 NLT)

God made everything, and God created you. He spoke, and it all came to be. You see, you are no accident, and you are no mistake. God knew you before you were born, and He has good plans for your life.

God is the creator, and He knows His creation best.

He knows how He made you, and He knows how you work. He knows what makes you happy and the things that make you feel sad. You are here on earth because God has a specific plan and purpose for you.

So, what does that mean for you and me? If God knows us best and He made it all, then today we can make a choice to follow His plan, His Word, His amazing life for us, His boundaries, and His voice. Your world and my world begin with the great and mighty One— God. He is the master chef who cooked up the wonderful miracle of you.

Daily Declaration:

I am God's daughter. I am a daughter of the King. He created me and says that I am very good. He knows me best.

Talking to God together:

God, thank you for creating everything, and thank you for making me. You are the master chef, and you are good. Help me change the way I think about the world and show me how to see you the right way. I ask that you guide me every day in your plan and purpose for my life. I love you, God.

Make a memory together:

Before bedtime, take a look outside or go outside and point out all your favorite things that God made.

Just for Dads: Elohim —
The One in Charge

There are certain days when you wake up before your alarm, ready and excited to go. As you get older, it seems those days can become fewer. I remember one day; I couldn't wait to hop out of bed and get moving. I got ready, hustled down the stairs, grabbed my guitar, and, for the first time ever, the keys to my dad's white Chevy pickup. That Sunday was my first time driving on the open road all by myself. I pulled onto the highway, feeling completely free, like I was in charge. Behind the wheel of that truck, I felt I could go anywhere I wanted.

When we read, "In the beginning God created the heavens and the earth" (Genesis 1:1 NIV), it can be easy to read quickly and move on: God created everything—got it. But what does that really mean? Here, the word for God is "Elohim," a Hebrew name meaning "supreme one" or "mighty one." It refers to the one true God, though the term is also used in the Bible for human rulers, judges, or angels—anyone displaying power or authority. So, in the beginning was the supreme one, the mighty one, the one truly in charge, who created it all. He created the entire universe and made you and me. As Creator, He set boundaries and spoke every creation into existence, down to the smallest cell in our bodies.

After creation, something remarkable happened. God gave human beings the gift of free will. Rather than making us robots, God desired sons and daughters who could freely choose to love or reject Him. It's almost as if God took the keys to our lives and handed them over to us. You and I step into the driver's seat of our Father's pickup truck that He saved for us, and we get to choose where to go and how to drive.

I can't pinpoint the exact moment I took control of my life and tried to be my own "god," but I can tell you it led to a lot of wreckage. Maybe it began in childhood when lying seemed easier than facing the pain of honesty, or maybe when I started listening to voices that seemed closer and more trustworthy than God's. Whether it was that or seeking momentary pleasure that clung to my mind like tar, I know what it feels like to take the wheel and try to be my own "supreme one."

I've learned that the best thing we can do with our free will is to surrender it to Jesus as Lord, trading our own will for His perfect one. I don't believe God will just take control of my beat-up Chevy pickup life without my surrender—that's not His way. But I do believe He speaks to us, guiding us like a GPS, step by step. Placing God back as our Elohim means surrendering to His plan, His word, His boundaries, His voice, and His rule in our lives.

My prayer for us as fathers today is that we put God back in His rightful place as the Elohim of our lives. This might mean surrendering your life to Him, confessing a hidden sin, placing a difficult situation in His hands, taking a step toward sobriety, asking forgiveness from someone you've hurt, or asking Him to humble you. Do whatever it takes to put Him back on the throne of your life.

"In the beginning the Word already existed. The Word was with God, and the Word was God."
John 1:1, NLT

Lesson 2:
Three in One

"The earth was formless and empty, and darkness covered the deep waters. And the Spirit of God was hovering over the surface of the waters." (Genesis 1:2, NLT)

Have you ever heard of a mystery? A mystery is something that is difficult or even impossible to explain. I want you to imagine yourself as a detective. What's your detective name? In today's mystery, we are diving into the puzzle of the 3 in 1. How can three different things be one thing?

Let's begin by looking at some clues together. We know that God the Father created everything. He made it all, including you and me. But in John 1:1 and Genesis 1:2, we learn that at the very beginning, God the Father wasn't alone. John says, "The Word was with God, and the Word was God." The Word is Jesus. At the very beginning of time, Jesus was with God, and Jesus was God. Not only was Jesus there, but in Genesis 1:2, it says, "And the Spirit of God was hovering over the surface of the waters."

Alright, detectives, at the very beginning, there was God the Father, there was Jesus, and there was the Spirit. We call this the Trinity. We have God the Father, Jesus the Son, and the Holy Spirit all present at the beginning, and together they created everything. You see, the Father, the Son, and the Holy Spirit are three different persons, but they are one powerful God. People have tried to explain how this works, but the truth is, it will always be a mystery. It'd be like trying to explain why your crazy Uncle Larry is so loony—that can never be explained. (We apologize to all the Uncle Larrys out there.)

This mystery of the three in one can be hard to understand, but it isn't hard to experience. God the Father loves you. He created you and formed you before you were ever in your momma's belly. God the Son loves you. He did something so unthinkable just so you and

I could be saved from the darkness in this world and in our own hearts. Jesus, the Son of God, made sure we could be children of God the Father. And the Holy Spirit is bringing you closer to Jesus. He is a helper for you, and when you and I make a bad choice, He shows us how to make it right and come back to the heart of God. The Holy Spirit gives you the power to live like Jesus and make a difference in this world.

Detective, I think we might have just cracked the case of the great 3 in 1. It's a mystery we will spend the rest of our lives learning more about.

In the meantime, talk to your Father in heaven, talk to Jesus, talk to the Holy Spirit, and see what great mysteries He has for you. Let's say this together: "Our God is 3 in 1. He is my Father, He is my Jesus, and He is the Holy Spirit."

Daily Declaration:

I am God's daughter. I am a daughter of the King. I believe in God the Father, I believe in Jesus the Son, and I believe in the Holy Spirit. My God is 3 in 1.

Talking to God together:

God, you are great! Some things about you are a mystery, and that is okay. I pray that I would live my life as a detective, discovering more about who you are. Help me to be more like Jesus by the power of the Holy Spirit.

Make a memory together:

Draw a picture together and hang it up on the fridge. In the picture, you will draw each other as a team of detectives. Don't forget to put your detective names on there. Whenever you pass by the picture, think about the great mystery of the Trinity.

"But the Lord God warned him,
'You may freely eat the fruit of
every tree in the garden- except the
tree of the knowledge of good and
evil. If you eat its fruit, you are
sure to die.'"

Genesis 2:16-17, NLT

Lesson 3:
A Not-So-Good Day

"The serpent was the shrewdest of all the wild animals the Lord God has made. One day he asked the woman, 'Did God really say you must not eat the fruit from any of the trees in the garden?'" (Genesis 3:1, NLT)

Have you ever had a not-so-good day? Maybe you had something really exciting happening at school, but you woke up sick, with a fever, throwing up last night's meatloaf. So instead of enjoying the great day at school, you had to lie down all day and miss out on the fun. Or maybe there was a time when someone said something really mean to you, and it was hard to get over. Stuff like that can make for a not-so-good day.

In the Bible, the first humans God created had some really good days. After God created everything, He made a beautiful garden called Eden. Eden means "heaven." This garden was incredible—it had animals, plants, flowers, and trees with so much delicious fruit. God made Adam and Eve. They were the first man and woman, and they were married. They probably kissed (yuck!). Adam and Eve lived in the Garden of Eden, and everything was perfect. There was no sickness, no bad days, and the whole world was theirs to discover without fear.

One day, Eve met a strange snake—a serpent, a loser dude. The snake asked Eve, "Did God really say you must not eat the fruit from any of the trees in the garden?"

Now, let's pause right here. God had made a LOT of trees, and those trees had a lot of fruit. God told Adam that he and Eve could eat from ANY tree they wanted, except for one. There was just one tree that was off-limits. God, the master chef, knew that if they ate from that one tree, it wouldn't be good. God created us, and He knows what is good for us and what will hurt us.

Back to our story: Eve is talking to the snake—who, by the way, is a total noodlehead. The snake tries to get Eve to eat the fruit. Do you think she does it? No, Eve, don't do it! Sadly, she eats the fruit. Not only that, but Adam was there too. He didn't stop her or even say anything. In fact, he ends up eating the fruit as well. In one moment, the perfect world God created fell apart. Adam and Eve broke it. This seems like a not-so-good day.

Because of Adam and Eve's choice, bad things came into the world, and God's great creation didn't seem so great anymore. Worst of all, Adam and Eve lost their close relationship with their Father, God. This is a tragedy, but that's not how the story ends. God still loved Adam and Eve, even after they made a bad choice. They faced some really hard consequences, but in the middle of that not so-good day, God made them a promise that changed everything. Whenever God makes a promise, you can bet He will keep it. God promised to send someone to save Adam, Eve, and all of humanity. We'll learn more about that soon.

It's easy to be mad at Adam and Eve and think, "You knuckle-heads, you ruined God's great world!" But the truth is, we all break the amazing things God has made. Whether it's telling a lie, saying something hurtful to a friend or family member, doing something we know is wrong, or stealing something that isn't ours, each of us has made choices that hurt the heart of God. This is called sin. The Bible says, "For everyone has sinned; we all fall short of God's glorious standard" (Romans 3:23 NLT). Each of us has made choices that aren't right.

Boy, this day seems kind of gloomy, huh? Well, here's some good news: In a world that is broken, God still loves you, me, and everyone He created. Don't forget—our God is 3 in 1. The Father,

Jesus the Son, and the Holy Spirit are all at work healing, rescuing, and bringing people back into a relationship with God.

Let's end this day on a good note. As the author, I say your dad should let you eat some ice cream before bed. (Sorry, dads!)

Daily Declaration:

I am God's daughter. I am a daughter of the King. My story will not end badly, because God has promised me a Savior.

Talking to God together:

God, even when things are not so good, You are still good. I ask today that You forgive me for my sin. Help me to live within Your boundaries. I love You, God.

Make a memory together:

Tonight before bed, eat a special treat together—just make sure it isn't the forbidden fruit!

Just for Dads: False Beliefs

The other day, my daughter was telling me about a little boy who likes her. Some of her classmates were teasing her for being kind to him. Of course, the dad in me had to choke down the urge to say, "Who does this little boy think he is?" and instead choose to be a decent human, pointing out that I was proud of her kindness.

This brought me back to when I was a kid. There was a girl who was "in love" with me, and she'd chase me all the time. One day, she even had her friends tackle me and hold me down so she could try to kiss me. Guess I was quite the charmer! I remember being so angry that I went home that night and prayed to God, asking Him to make her stop chasing me and liking me. The next day, to my surprise, she wasn't at school. In my young mind, I thought, "Wow, God really heard me!" But then I found out she'd been in a car accident. I was horrified and couldn't shake the feeling that my prayer had somehow caused her to get hurt. I believed it was all my fault.

At the time, I didn't understand, but I now know that thinking my prayer caused God to harm her was a major false belief. God doesn't cause injury or suffering, nor is He the kind of God who gives anyone sickness or tragedy. In our broken world, these things happen, and sometimes He allows us to walk through challenges, but my prayer didn't make a good God turn bad or hurt that girl.

It might seem like a silly story now, and sometimes I laugh at myself when I think back on it. But the truth is, we all carry ideas, beliefs, and assumptions about God that simply aren't true. I love how Michael Dye puts it in his workbook The Genesis Process: "What you do comes out of your beliefs about yourself, others, and God. In order to have a new life, not just a change of destructive behaviors, you must examine your current belief systems."

As I began a journey of addressing some of the harder parts of my life, examining my beliefs about myself, others, and God became a doorway to discovering what's true. I'm reminded of Paul's words in

Romans 12:2: "Don't copy the behavior and customs of this world, but let God transform you into a new person by changing the way you think. Then you will learn to know God's will for you, which is good and pleasing and perfect." When we cling to false beliefs, we allow ourselves to be pressed into molds that weren't meant for us. We become negative, wear masks, strive to be "good" or hide our struggles, and may even become the people we once swore we'd never be. It all starts with the cracks in our belief systems.

When we take a journey to uncover the truth about God, ourselves, and the world around us, we give God permission to shape and mold us instead of being forced into someone else's mold. He begins to transform each false belief, tearing down lies and showing us who we really are in Him. If you've experienced pain or abuse, that doesn't make you broken or worthless—you are God's child. If you've believed the lie that you need money or fame to be worthy, God shows us a better way. We begin to see Him as He is—our Father, Jesus Christ our Savior, and the Holy Spirit.

God loves you and wants to be close to you. He wants to offer you grace, freedom, and a life free from lies. I'm praying today that God will break down those false beliefs and show you what's true.

"...He will strike your head, and you will strike his heel."

Genesis 3:15 NLT

Lesson 4:
The Promised Hero

For just a moment, let's pretend we're somewhere else. Imagine we're at Disneyland! Picture yourself walking through the gates into a world full of flowers, with light music that makes your heart feel happy. You're so joyful that you start skipping! You're wearing a cute Disneyland shirt and sparkly Minnie Mouse ears—you look totally fabulous, and you know it. As you stroll through what feels like the happiest place on Earth, bubbles float in the air, and the smell of churros and other sweet treats fill your nose. Your dad feels lighter too—probably because all those treats helped him get rid of some money weighing down his pockets. In the distance, you notice a random kid crying in a stroller. He doesn't understand the magic yet, but we'll pray for him!

Now, think about getting on a ride that transports you into your favorite movie. You're so excited to jump on, but suddenly, something stops you. The line to the ride stretches out longer than a billion churros! The last thing you want to do is wait, but it's the only way to get on your beloved ride. I'm sorry, I might have just messed up our Disneyland dream with that!

Waiting can be tough when the thing you're waiting for is exciting or important. Whether it's waiting for dinner, summer vacation, or your dad letting you have a boyfriend (you'll be waiting until you're 35, young lady!), we can all agree—waiting is hard!

Now, let's travel to a different place than Disneyland. Imagine you lived back when the Bible was written. The people of God, the Israelites, were waiting for something very important. After Adam and Eve sinned, God promised to send a hero—someone who would defeat evil and fix what had been broken. They were waiting for the one who would crush the head of that big-time loser snake, Satan (Genesis 3:15).

Years passed, and God's people were still waiting. Prophets began to speak about this promised hero, saying that He would come from the tribe of Judah (Genesis 49:10). One prophet said He would be a leader like Moses, who would speak God's words and deliver His people (Deuteronomy 18:15). Another said He would be born in a small town called Bethlehem (Micah 5:2). A prophet named Isaiah even said that this hero would suffer, and by His wounds, we would be healed (Isaiah 53:5).

But despite all these promises, God's people kept waiting. Some obeyed God while they waited, but many didn't, which was pretty sad. Hundreds, maybe thousands, of years passed, and still, no hero had come.

Then, one amazing day, a baby boy was born in Bethlehem to a young virgin named Mary. His name was Jesus. Not many people realized it at the time, but this little boy might just be the promised hero— the one everyone had been waiting for. He would grow up and maybe, just maybe, be the hero that would crush the head of the snake. We'll learn more about Jesus tomorrow, but for now, we'll just have to wait.

Daily Declaration:

I am God's daughter. I am a daughter of the King. I believe what the Bible says, and I believe that Jesus is the hero God promised. I will spend my whole life learning more about who Jesus is.

Talking to God Together:

Jesus, thank You for being the hero of the world and my own personal hero. I ask that You would make me into someone who boldly shares

Pizza Notes

Pizza Notes

INDEX

ACKNOWLEDGMENTS

This book took a village to produce, and I'm grateful to every friend, family member, colleague, and reader who helped shepherd my idea from brainstorm to finished files.

SPECIAL THANKS TO:

JOANNA AND DANIELLE, for understanding my vision and transforming it into something way cooler than I could have imagined

JESS, for her friendship and editorial prowess

JOHN AND JACK, for never getting tired of homemade pizza

THE TNP PIZZA BRAIN TRUST, for responding to polls, sharing pizza-making woes, and weighing in on design and content ideas

THURSDAY NIGHT PIZZA READERS, whose comments and questions inspired every part of this book

... AND ALL THE PEOPLE WHO'VE ASKED, "Will you ever run out of pizza ideas?"—I hope, by now, you know the answer.

ABOUT THE AUTHOR

Peggy Paul Casella is a recipe developer, writer, cookbook consultant, and homemade pizza enthusiast based in Philadelphia. Her website, ThursdayNightPizza.com, hosts the largest selection of original pizza and pizza-related recipes on the Internet, and her other cookbooks include the *Teenage Mutant Ninja Turtles Pizza Cookbook* (Insight Editions, 2017) and *The Dip Deck* (Clarkson Potter, 2025).

To learn more about Peggy and her work, visit PeggyPaulCasella.com.

PeggyPaulCasella

www.ingramcontent.com/pod-product-compliance
Lightning Source LLC
Chambersburg PA
CBHW051309120626
46547CB00015B/2161

Your story with others. I love You and can't wait to learn more about You. Amen.

Make a Memory Together:

Take some time today to plan your dream vacation together. Where would you go? What would it be like? Use your imagination, and remember that the best things in life are worth waiting for.

"Jesus grew in wisdom and in stature and in favor with God and all the people."

Luke 2:52, NLT

Lesson 5:

What a Life!

"For this is how God loved the world: He gave his one and only Son, so that everyone who believes in him will not perish but have eternal life. God sent his Son into the world not to judge the world, but to save the world through him." (John 3:16-17, NLT)

Your dad probably has the incredible gift of being a fixer. I bet he can fix just about anything that breaks around your house. I can already picture him hammering in screws and drilling in nails! My daughters, on the other hand, aren't as lucky. I can't fix anything at our house. I've tried fixing small things, big things—you name it. And every time, I somehow manage to make it worse than when I started. So, if you're a dad who can't fix things, just know we're in this together! And if you can fix things, how much would you charge to fix my dishwasher? (I'm asking for a friend.)

The truth is, we all have things we're not the best at. And one thing we all have in common is that we aren't perfect at life. You might say, "What?! I'm crushing life, thank you very much." But hear me out. The Bible says in 1 John 1:8, "If we claim to be without sin, we deceive ourselves and the truth is not in us." That might sound harsh, but it's true. We all mess up. We all have moments where we fall short of God's best for us, and sometimes, we make pretty big mistakes.

God's people, the Israelites, were no different. They sinned against God and broke His heart. There was a system where they tried to follow God's laws, but every time they sinned (and they sinned a lot!), they had to sacrifice animals as payment for their sin. Since the cost of sin is death, an innocent animal had to die because people weren't living the right way. It sounds unfair, right?

Fast forward a lot of years, and a little baby is born—Jesus, the promised hero. Jesus grows up, and the Bible says in Luke 2:52, "Jesus grew in wisdom and in stature and in favor with God and all the people." You see, Jesus wasn't just good at life; He lived the perfect life. He showed great wisdom, and every choice He made was pleasing to His Father in heaven. Jesus grew up, became a teacher of God's Law, and was known as a Rabbi—a great honor. He was different from others, and when He spoke, people listened. At the age of 30, Jesus began His ministry. As a Rabbi, He chose 12 disciples who didn't seem like the best choice, but Jesus chose them and poured His life into them. God was with Jesus, and He was full of the Holy Spirit. It can be a little confusing, but Jesus was fully God and fully man. He hung out with people who were sick, who were hurting, and He spent time with those others had given up on. Jesus healed the broken and always followed His Father's voice.

God's people weren't great at life, but Jesus stepped in and lived a perfect one. Just like us, God's people made poor choices, but when we look at the life of Jesus, we see an example we can follow. God the Father loved the world so much that He didn't want anyone to die for their sins or be far from Him. So He sent His Son, Jesus. Jesus didn't come to yell at people or be mean to them—

He came to save the hurting, and He lived an innocent and perfect life. You may not be great at some things, and that's totally okay. You may have made some choices that weren't the best, but there's someone who was tempted in every way like we are, yet never sinned. His name is Jesus. Some thought He was just a good man, while others began to believe He was the hero God had promised.

What do you think?

Daily Declaration:

I am God's daughter. I am a daughter of the King. I believe that Jesus is Lord. He is the hero God promised to all of mankind. I will follow Jesus all the days of my life.

Talking to God Together:

Jesus, you are the son of God and because of You we have victory. I pray that when I am tempted to sin, I would remember that You are my example of how to live. I want to live with Jesus as my teacher.

Make a Memory Together:

Build something together! Whether it's a fort, a birdhouse, or a Lego tower, create something fun—and if you want, wreck it! But if you build a masterpiece, definitely don't wreck it.

"But Jesus remained silent. Then the high priest said to him, 'I demand in the name of the living God- tell us if you are the Messiah, the Son of God.' Jesus replied, 'You have said it. And in the future, you will see the Son of Man seated in the place of power at God's right hand and coming on the clouds of heaven.'"

Matthew 26:63-64, NLT

Lesson 6:

The Decision

Jesus told her "I am the resurrection and the life. Anyone who believes in me will live, even after dying." (John 11:25, NLT)

I've heard it said, "You can tell a lot about someone based on their shoes." A person walks up, and based on the kind of kicks they're wearing, you get a sense of who they are. So, I wonder, could you tell a lot about Jesus based on the sandals He wore? They were probably pretty beat up from all the adventures He went on— covered in dirt, mud, maybe with parts starting to tear, or colors faded from rain and all of the miles He walked. If Jesus walked up to us, we might see His shoes and think, "He's poor," or, "He doesn't take great care of those chanclas (sandals)." Someone who didn't know Him might even decide He wasn't worth getting to know based on those dirty sandals.

But if you knew the story behind those muddy, torn shoes you would see that those sandals had been through a lot! One time, Jesus fed 5,000 men—plus a whole lot more women and children— with those sandals on His feet. He used just five loaves of bread and two fish, prayed over them, and fed a huge crowd. Another time, those sandals were soaked in a violent storm while the disciples screamed, "We're gonna die!" when, all of a sudden, Jesus calmed the whole storm with a simple sentence. Those sandals had walked through the roughest parts of town, waiting patiently while Jesus had dinner and hung out with friends. They'd heard jokes from Jesus, maybe even joined in on a prank or two He played on His friends. They had walked miles just to help someone in need. Knowing all that, what do those dirty sandals tell you about Jesus?

The most important question you and I will ever answer is this: who do you say Jesus is? After hearing, learning, and experiencing, who do you think He is? It all comes down to a decision. Does the man wearing those sandals fit the description of the promised hero?

One night, Jesus was with His disciples, saying goodbye to them. His disciples were confused because they didn't want Jesus to leave. Soon after, Jesus was betrayed by one of His friends and taken to trial, even though He'd done nothing wrong. Another friend totally disowned Him, saying, "I don't even know Him." A crowd yelled, "Crucify Him!" More and more people began to think the man in those sandals was nothing but trouble. Jesus was treated horribly and hurt in ways we can barely imagine. They took Him and nailed Him to a cross. It was almost as if everyone had decided that Jesus didn't matter. Jesus looked out at the crowd of people and those who were hurting Him, and He told His Father in Heaven, "Forgive them, for they know not what they do." He breathed His final breath, and the chances of Jesus being the promised hero seemed to be all but lost.

But wait! Hold on just one minute. We're getting reports that the grave Jesus was placed in is empty. The man with the dirty sandals is RISEN. You see, Jesus not only died but the power of God raised Him from the dead! This is literally the most important and amazing day in history. The promised hero beat death and conquered sin forever! Jesus ended up being the promised hero. Jesus is more than a good guy, a cool teacher, or a popular person—He is the Son of God, and He is God!

Now, the decision is up to you. Who do you say Jesus is? Is He just another guy? Or is Jesus the Lord of your life? Is He your leader, your Savior, your friend—the hero God promised you? Today, if you make the decision to make Jesus your Lord and hero, then your dad will be able to lead you in a prayer together.

Instructions for Dads:

Ask your daughter(s) this question...

Q: Do you want to make Jesus your Lord and hero today? If your daughter(s) said yes, pray this with them:

Jesus, I have made choices that aren't the best. Today, I ask for Your forgiveness. I believe that You are the promised hero, that You died for my sins and rose again. Today, I am deciding to make You my Lord. I will walk with You all the days of my life. Thank You for Your love, and thank You for being my hero. Amen.

Make a Memory Together:

Grab your favorite pair of shoes and ask each other, "What do my shoes tell you about me?" Maybe the answers will be silly, maybe a few insults will get tossed around about our awesome dad shoes, or maybe some answers will be pretty surprising (hopefully in a good way!).

"The earth was formless and empty, and darkness covered the deep waters. And the Spirit of God was hovering over the surface of the waters."
Genesis 1:2, NLT

Lesson 7:
A Place To Rest

"After his baptism, as Jesus came up out of the water, the heavens were opened, and he saw the Spirit of God descending like a dove and settling on him." (Matthew 3:16, NLT)

"But you will receive power when the Holy Spirit comes upon you. And you will be my witnesses, telling people about me everywhere— in Jerusalem, throughout Judea, in Samaria, and to the ends of the earth." (Acts of the Apostles 1:8, NLT)

There once was a dove named Glory. Glory was beautiful and strong. This incredible dove would spend time flying and hovering over the spaces God the Father had created. Glory and the Father were one, and Glory was a carrier of the Father's greatness. Being close to Glory meant being close to the Father. In the beginning, Glory lingered in the darkness, and when God made the Garden of Eden, Glory spent time with Adam and Eve. Everywhere Glory went, there was peace and joy.

Then, one terrible day in the garden, everything changed. Glory felt sad, but just like the Father, Glory never stopped staying close to the world God had created. The Father's plan was for Glory to have a place to rest, a place to call home. As time went on, Glory had a few different homes. Glory helped some of God's people do incredible things, spending time with kings, guiding God's people through tough times, and even residing in a box called the Ark of the Covenant. Glory rested in a beautiful tabernacle and a magnificent temple. Everyone wanted

Glory nearby, but the right home hadn't been reached quite yet. Sometimes, people mistreated Glory by disobeying the Father in heaven.

One day, an unusual man named John the Baptist was leading people back to God and baptizing them in a river called the Jordan. A man named Jesus arrived, and John knew that Jesus was the promised Hero. That day, John baptized Jesus, and as Jesus rose from the water, Glory came and rested on Him. Glory had found a home. Jesus and Glory were the closest of friends, and together, they followed God's great plan for Jesus. Throughout Jesus' life, He remained in the presence of Glory, listening and staying connected.

When Jesus died on the cross, it was Glory's power that raised Him from the dead. Jesus wanted all His disciples to experience what it was like to have Glory as their helper, close beside them. After Jesus rose from the dead, He told His friends to wait, promising to send them someone who would be with them always. Jesus was going to send Glory. The disciples and some other believers gathered and waited, praying and anticipating. Then, suddenly, the Holy Spirit arrived, filling the whole room and each disciple. They began to speak in other languages, and on that day, the church was born.

This little story about Glory is a way to help us understand more about the Holy Spirit. The Holy Spirit lives inside every believer, filling us with His presence and power. The Holy Spirit is a person, and He is God. You and I have the opportunity to live led by the Holy Spirit every day.

Daily Declaration:

I am God's daughter, a daughter of the King. The Holy Spirit lives in me and gives me power to live like Jesus. I will live every day by the power of God's Spirit.

Talking to God Together:

Holy Spirit, I ask that you fill me with your power today. I thank you that you would send Your Spirit to live inside of me. Holy Spirit you are welcome in my life.

Make a Memory Together:

Pick your favorite worship song and find a way to play it. Spend a moment together tonight worshipping God. Lift your hands and invite the Holy Spirit to be the helper who fills your home and your heart.

"But in fact, it is best for you that I go away, because if I don't, the Advocate won't come. If I do go away, then I will send him to you. And when he comes, he will convict the world of its sin, and of God's righteousness, and of the coming judgment."

John 16:7-8, NLT

Lesson 8:
Hamburger Helper

"And I will ask the Father, and he will give you another Advocate, who will never leave you. He is the Holy Spirit, who leads into all truth. The world cannot receive him, because it isn't looking for him and doesn't recognize him. But you know him, because he lives with you now and later will be in you." (John 14:16-17, NLT)

Growing up, one of my favorite dinners my mom would make was the delicious, decadent, and divine delicacy known as Hamburger Helper. First, you chop up an onion and toss it into a hot pan with a bit of oil, letting it start sweating like a dad mowing the lawn on a hot summer day. Once the onion has cooked down, you add in a pound of ground beef. In my opinion, ground beef is the most basic of all the delicious beef cuts out there. Once it's all browned and broken up, you've got hamburger meat. But how do you take simple, everyday ground beef and turn it into something magical? That's where the box of Hamburger Helper comes in. Whether it's the Lasagna flavor, the Stroganoff, or the crunchy taco, each of those Hamburger Helper boxes takes basic ol' beef and helps it become a masterpiece.

While Jesus was on earth, He promised us a Helper. He said He would send someone named the Holy Spirit. The Holy Spirit is the third person of the Trinity—Father, Son, and Holy Spirit. The Holy Spirit is a person, and He is God. God the Father sent His Son into the world, and Jesus, the Son, promised to send the Spirit to live inside of us. Jesus actually said it would be better for Him to leave so He could send us the Holy Spirit.

The Holy Spirit plays a vital role in our lives. Every person who has chosen to make Jesus their Lord and hero has the Holy Spirit living within them, helping regular, everyday people become more like Jesus. He takes us in our ground-beef-level basicness and helps us become the masterpiece God created us to be. Sometimes, we may feel like having a relationship with God is difficult, or that He feels distant, but the truth is, God lives inside of us. This is an incredible miracle to know that God Himself would come and live inside of little ol' you and me. The Holy Spirit shows us when we've messed up and leads us back to God's heart without making us feel shame. He encourages us, speaks life over us, and gives us the power to live for Jesus.

Every day, the Holy Spirit is our leader and our Helper, making all the difference in our lives. You are on a journey becoming the young person God has created you to be and The Holy Spirit is leading that adventure.

Daily Declaration:

I am God's daughter, a daughter of the King. Holy Spirit, you are my helper, and you give me the power to live like Jesus. I will live in the presence of the Holy Spirit each day.

Talking to God Together:

Holy Spirit, I thank you that you are God and that you are at work in our world and within each of us. We ask that we would be a family that follows you and leans into your presence and power within us. We need you, Holy Spirit.

Make a Memory Together:

Tonight is a fun one! Plan a daddy-daughter date together. Keep the plan because you are going to need it in the coming days of our journey.

Just for Dads: Full of It

"But you will receive power when the Holy Spirit comes upon you. And you will be my witnesses, telling people about me everywhere— in Jerusalem, throughout Judea, in Samaria, and to the ends of the earth." (Acts of the Apostles 1:8 NLT)

Back in high school, I always looked up to these two senior guys. They benched more than anyone, had the most girlfriends, and were stars on the football field and basketball court. Watching them made me wish I wasn't just a short, husky freshman. As time went on, I watched these two incredible senior dudes become the most normal, completely unimpressive adults. Sometimes, I think the lucky streak can just run out for some people. And if I'm honest, I've been around long enough to know that no man is perfect. I think each of us eventually runs out of that manly heroicness. Whether it's men I really looked up to making a poor decision, or my own failures taking a big chunk out of my confidence, every man I've ever met has weaknesses and needs the help of someone greater than himself.

After Jesus had risen, He was hanging out with His disciples, giving them words of life and instructions because He'd soon be leaving them. His promise of the Holy Spirit must've felt pretty important. These super ordinary, unimpressive disciples suddenly found their lives turned exciting with Jesus around. Without Him, would they be enough to carry out instructions like, "Go into all the world and make disciples, baptizing them in the name of the Father, the Son, and the Holy Spirit?" Peter seemed like a cool guy, but I don't think he had what it takes to carry out an order like that. But when the Holy Spirit came upon the disciples and those in the upper room, those ordinary people became the church. A bunch of broken people became the body of believers who would carry out a mission so impossible that some of them would go on to die for the Gospel.

This might be a little tough to hear, but, my friend, you and I aren't enough. As much as I'd like to be the hero of my story, the great prince charming for my wife, and the ultimate provider and protector for my children—I simply am not enough. I wish my gifts could open every door, and my witty words make a way for me, but I simply am not enough. That's not putting myself down—it's simply the truth. You and I need the Holy Spirit. We need God Himself to move into our lives and live within us. We need His voice for direction, His conviction to break us down in the most beautiful way so we can look like Jesus, and we need the power of the Holy Spirit within us just to make it through the day in this broken and difficult world.

Each of us is full of something. Maybe you're full of anger, or full of pride, or maybe, like me, sometimes you're just full of crap. Whatever you're full of, I think it's time to allow yourself to be full of the Holy Spirit. When the Holy Spirit comes upon you, you receive power. This power changes you for good. This power is for you, and God desires to fill you.

Today, I am believing that you will be filled with the Holy Spirit. Some of you today will receive your heavenly prayer language, and others of you will find peace for the difficulty you may be facing in your mind. The Holy Spirit will take your life and use you to be a witness—in your home, with your wife, to your children, with your neighbor, with your co-worker, and every place God takes you. Be filled with the Holy Spirit, dad! May His power and presence surround you right now and change you from the inside out.

"Now the Lord is the Spirit, and where the Spirit of the Lord is, there is freedom. And we all, who with unveiled faces contemplate the Lord's glory, are being transformed into his image with ever increasing glory, which comes from the Lord, who is the Spirit."

2 Corinthians 3:17-18, NLT

Lesson 9:

Filled with Fruit

"But the Holy Spirit produces this kind of fruit in our lives: love, joy, peace, patience, kindness, goodness, faithfulness, gentleness, and self-control. There is no law against these things!" (Galatians 5:22-23, NLT)

When I was little, I had a really weird fear. In my parents' kitchen, my mom kept a fruit basket on the counter. It was full of oranges, apples, bananas, peaches, nectarines, and my favorite—an occasional prapple (pear apple). Try them; they're pretty delicious. Every time the basket was full of fruit, I felt confident, like our family had enough to make it through the week. When the fruit basket was full, I felt blessed. But as the week went on and we ate the fruit, anxiety started to grow in me. The moment the last piece was gone, I'd become fearful, thinking we no longer had anything. To me, an empty fruit basket meant "no more blessing." My mom would go to the store and restock the apples, and just like that, our family was blessed again. Let's be honest, I was a weird kid.

The Holy Spirit wants to do incredible things in your life. He wants to fill you with His presence and produce His fruit in you. You and I are like the fruit basket on my mom's counter. If we choose not to live by the Spirit, we end up empty, with no fruit to be found—and that is a reason to worry. When we're filled with the Spirit, we're filled with a person. We're filled with God Himself. God comes in, giving us gifts. He may give us a heavenly prayer language, comfort us, and begin to change things in our hearts and lives that don't look like Jesus. The Holy Spirit wants to fill you.

Not only that, but the Spirit produces fruit in our lives. Our basket starts to carry the sweet taste of love for others, or maybe our life starts to have the tang of God's joy where before there was only sadness. The Spirit can give us all the nutrients of peace and patience. Imagine you're a little loco in all the wrong ways, and suddenly your life starts to "drip drip" with the delicious flavors of goodness, faithfulness, gentleness, and self-control. The Holy Spirit produces fruit in our lives. It's a beautiful image. Jesus, the Son of God, is the vine that gives us life; God the Father is the gardener who tends to us and cares for us; and the Holy Spirit is at work in all of it so that we can produce fruit and be filled with God Himself.

On this journey of being a daughter of the King, you're becoming someone extraordinary. You are no insignificant part of this world. You're a vital and wonderful masterpiece that God wants to fill with His Spirit. You're becoming His daughter who will make a huge impact in His Kingdom.

Daily Declaration:

I am God's daughter, a daughter of the King. I am filled with the Spirit and He is producing fruit in me.

Talking to God Together:

Holy Spirit, fill me today with your power and your fruit. I need more of the Holy Spirit in my life.

Make a Memory Together:

Before bed tonight lay hands on your daughter(s) and pray that the Holy Spirit would fill them up with His love, presence, and power.

"For I know the plans I have for you," says the Lord. "They are plans for good and not for disaster, to give you a future and a hope. In those days when you pray, I will listen. If you look for me wholeheartedly, you will find me. I will be found by you," says the Lord. "I will end your captivity and restore your fortunes. I will gather you out of the nations where I sent you and will bring you home again to your own land."

Jeremiah 29:11-14, NLT

Lesson 10:
The Declaration

Say this together out loud:

"I believe in God the Father,
the Creator of heaven and earth;
and in Jesus Christ, His only Son, my Lord,
who was conceived by the Holy Spirit,
born of the Virgin Mary.
He suffered for me, was crucified, died, and was buried;
He descended to the dead.
On the third day, He rose again;
He ascended into heaven,
is seated at the right hand of the Father,
and will come again.
I believe in the Holy Spirit,
the Church,
the communion of saints,
the forgiveness of sins,
the resurrection of the body,
and the life everlasting. Amen."

Being a daughter of the King begins by knowing who our King is. He is more than the big guy in the sky or a God that is far away in heaven. Our God is close, He is all powerful, everywhere, all the time, and He loves you and me so much. He is 3 in 1 and He has good plans for your life. God led Jeremiah to write these verses after God's people were led into a difficult situation. God allowed them to walk through something hard and He is reminding them that in the midst of this hard thing He is still good, He is in control, and His plans for them are good. No matter what you are facing never forget that God has a good plan for your life. You can count on that for the rest of your life.

Make a Memory Together:

Today, dad gets to pick a game or activity to do together. Maybe he wants to shoot some hoops? Or maybe he wants you to help him wash the dishes? Whatever dad chooses, the daughters have to participate.

Part Two:

Who Am I?

The Daddy Daughter Date

To accomplish this day, you'll need to make some time to take your daughter(s) on a date. It doesn't need to be an expensive one, but it's important that we, as dads, do our best to connect with our girls. During the date, take a moment to go through Lesson 11 together.

Maybe you get all dressed up and go to McDonald's and the park, or perhaps you have a picnic in the front yard. If your girl(s) are anything like mine, they'll probably ask to go get some ice cream!

As we begin the second part of our journey, we'll be focusing on identity. One of the most powerful sources of identity for a young person is their dad. You're a good dad, laying a solid foundation for your daughter(s) to walk on. Go out and make a memory together. I am cheering you on!

Just for Dads: Breaking the Pattern

"You must not bow down to them or worship them, for I, the Lord your God, am a jealous God who will not tolerate your affection for any other gods. I lay the sins of the parents upon their children; the entire family is affected—even children in the third and fourth generations of those who reject me. But I lavish unfailing love for a thousand generations on those who love me and obey my commands." (Deuteronomy 5:9-10, NLT)

When I first became interested in learning more about the Bible, I started at the beginning in Genesis. It didn't take long before I noticed a pattern that really stood out to me.

There's this guy named Abraham, and one day, out of fear for his life, he asks his wife to pretend to be his sister. If I'm honest, I don't think a trick like that would work with my wife. She'd be like, "Heck no, that's weird."

Abraham has a son named Isaac, and suddenly—out of nowhere in the storyline—Isaac ends up in the same situation and tells the exact same lie. That was kind of weird to me. Then comes Isaac's son, Jacob, and rather than just telling a lie, his very name literally means "deceiver"—and his entire life seems to be one long series of tricks and lies.

I'm no FBI agent, but there's clearly a pattern of broken behavior running through this family.

A theme we see in Scripture is that family lines carry both patterns of brokenness and patterns of blessing. The truth is, every single one of us lives with a certain level of wounds that come from our earthly fathers. Whether your father was absent, abusive, or present, we all carry some kind of hurt because we've been raised by imperfect, broken men.

For me, I grew up hearing stories about my dad's father—the brokenness he brought into my dad's life and the harm it caused.

But one day, when I was about four years old, my dad—the

product of a not-so-good situation—decided to make Jesus his Lord and Savior.

And in that very moment, the trajectory of our entire family line changed. A complete 180-degree turn.

Now, I wish I could say that because of my dad's decision, I grew up without any father wounds. But the truth is, I have my own set of things to work through. However, there's one major difference in my life because of a family surrendered to Jesus:

The process of sanctification—the lifelong journey of becoming more like Jesus—must run its course in every single person. No matter how radical someone's salvation story is, we are all on a journey and have things in us that still need work.

But because my family surrendered to Jesus, our stories came under the hand and guidance of a Father who never lets go. A Father who will never hurt us. And instead of leaving us with wounds that scar us, this Father sent His only Son to take on our wounds—the ones we rightfully deserved because of our own brokenness.

And in return, He traded our filth for His perfect plan.

I don't know your story. I don't know what kind of wounds you carry from your earthly father. But I can guarantee you this:

Every wound can be traded—for a sound mind, for a testimony of victory, for a new generational pattern of blessing—as you submit to the Lordship of Jesus.

There are incredible kiddos out there who, more than any gift or amount of care you could give them, desperately need you to leave them the generational pattern of being a Christ-follower.

As badly as I want to turn from the filth of my past and become a new man, I know that my children will still grow up with some level of father wounds—because I am imperfect. But because of my dad's decision to follow Jesus, which came from a praying mom who believed that her high school sweetheart could be saved, a broken family line received a new Father.

You got this, Dad.

Lead your kids into a new kind of pattern.

A pattern of addiction can become a pattern of restoration as you walk in recovery. A pattern of performance-based living can become a new generation of Christ-followers who know their identity doesn't come from what they do—but from who they are in Jesus.

How will your family line change because of your decision to follow Jesus?

"So God created human beings in his own image. In the image of God he created them; male and female he created them."
Genesis 1:27, NLT

Lesson 11:

I Am God's Daughter

Have you ever taken a selfie before? Maybe you're like me, and you see people around you taking random selfies. You chuckle to yourself (hopefully not out loud!) because, let's be honest, sometimes they look a little silly. Getting the perfect selfie can be tricky—you have to nail the pose, make sure the smile is bright, and decide if you're going for duck lips or a fierce look. As a dad of four daughters, I've definitely come across my fair share of selfies from my girls on my phone.

Now, here's a question that might sound a little strange, but stay with me—what do you think a selfie of God would look like? If you sent God a text and asked Him to send a selfie, what would you expect to get back? This is totally just my opinion, but I don't think we'd get an actual picture. I don't imagine God would give us duck lips or a fierce smolder and send it our way. Instead, in scripture, we see that God created human beings in His own image. It's as if He wanted to give us a glimpse of who He is through His creation. So, He handcrafted humans, placed His image in us, breathed life into us, and put us on display for His glory.

Think about it: God wanted to show the world a picture of Himself, so He created us—that includes you. Sure, sin broke that image, but Jesus came to fix it. Every person who calls upon the name of Jesus has that image restored and is continually being transformed back into the likeness of Christ.

So, if we asked God for a picture of Himself, I think He'd show a picture of you. He'd say, "This is my daughter, created in my image. She's beautiful, she's joyful, and she brings delight to my heart. She's the apple of my eye." God would smile with pride, His eyes welling up with tears as He looked at your face. He'd probably tell a story about when you were little and share just how proud He is of who you've become. The Father would say, "My Son, Jesus, lives in her. She is clean, forgiven, chosen, and set apart for My glory." He'd point out that the Holy Spirit dwells in you, making you strong, brave, wise, and full of God's power.

God can see so much in you, His daughter, from just one little image—an image that we might overlook. He's not pointing out your flaws or making you feel like you don't measure up. Today, the Father says, "You are my daughter, created in my image." You reflect your Father in heaven. Everything good in Him, He's placed in you. In a broken world, sin and temptation might cloud that image, but it's still there. You are God's daughter, and you are loved more deeply than you could ever imagine.

Daily Declaration:

I am God's daughter, a daughter of the King. I am loved and chosen by my Father in Heaven.

Talking to God Together:

God, we thank You that we are Your children. Today, we pray that we would never forget Your love for us and that You have chosen us. Help us to grow every day to reflect more of the image of Jesus that You've placed in us.

Make a Memory Together:

Take a selfie together! Duck lips? Fierce face? Big smiles? Silly picture? Snap some photos together, and maybe even print them out to keep.

"You made all the delicate, inner parts of my body and knit me together in my mother's womb. Thank you for making me so wonderfully complex! Your workmanship is marvelous—how well I know it. You watched me as I was being formed in utter seclusion, as I was woven together in the dark of the womb. You saw me before I was born. Every day of my life was recorded in your book. Every moment was laid out before a single day had passed. How precious are your thoughts about me, O God. They cannot be numbered! I can't even count them; they outnumber the grains of sand! And when I wake up, you are still with me!"
Psalms 139:13-18, NLT

Lesson 12:
I Was Made Very Good

I used to work as a line cook at a restaurant that served a lot of burgers and fries. I loved hearing the ticket box start printing a brand-new order. The head cook would call out the tickets, and if the station I was working at got called, I'd get the chance to craft my very own greasy culinary masterpiece.

One time, I was cooking for someone who seemed pretty important in our small town. I had to get this order perfect. I threw two beautiful slices of buttermilk bread on the griddle, basted them with just the right amount of butter to get that golden, crispy crust, and placed three slices of cheese to melt while I sautéed some ham. This was going to be the ultimate grilled ham-and-cheese masterpiece. I pulled the finished product off the grill, sliced it, and plated it with some hot, fresh fries. This order was ready to go to the VIP guest.

I felt so proud—until about four minutes later when the waitress brought the plate back and said a few words that almost ruined my day: "This was made wrong!"

What? How? I knew that sandwich was perfect! Little did I know there was a slice of paper stuck between the slices of ham that I hadn't noticed. My celebrity guest took a bite and ate straight-up paper. What a tragedy!

Mistakes happen—it's a part of life. But one thing that will never be a mistake is the way God made you. There may be times when you look in the mirror and aren't entirely happy with certain things about yourself. But the Bible teaches us that God created us, knit us together, and made us His masterpiece. He made every part of you, and you are no mistake.

Whether your hair is curly or straight, whether you're tall or short, whether you have adorable freckles or precious dimples when you smile—you are fearfully, wonderfully, and beautifully made.

God designed you to be a gorgeous young woman who will make an impact for His Kingdom. We all have moments of wondering if we're good enough or if we were made "right." But God created male and female, and you, my beautiful daughter(s), are God's masterpiece. You were made very good.

When you look in the mirror, I want you to say, "I was made wonderful and beautiful in every single way." Your Father in Heaven loves you, and you bring a smile to His face. Young daughter, not a single thing about you is out of place. You can trust God's Word because it's right and true, and when He said you were made very good, that's the only thing you need to believe about you.

Daily Declaration:

I am God's daughter, a daughter of the King. I am fearfully and wonderfully made.

Talking to God Together:

Lord, thank You for making us and for calling us very good. We ask today that we would see ourselves through Your eyes, and that no lie about how we were made or any doubt about us would get in the way of the truth that we are Your handiwork. We love You, and we thank You for who You are. Amen.

Make a Memory Together:

Tonight, grab a washable marker and head to your bathroom mirror. At the top, write: I was made very good. You can even add some positive adjectives that describe you! Words like beautiful, funny, smart, and kind are great examples that perfectly fit you. And don't forget—make sure your dad has the same thing written where he gets ready, with positive adjectives that describe him just right too!

"For we are God's masterpiece. He has created us anew in Christ Jesus, so we can do the good things he planned for us long ago."
Ephesians 2:10, NLT

Lesson 13:
I Was Created to Make a Difference

Let's play a little game. I'll name a few items, and your task is to say what the purpose of those items is. What do they do? Let's start with a hairbrush—what does a hairbrush do? Next up, we have the great and mighty ice cream scoop. What does that do? How about a camera?

Now, it may seem pretty simple to figure out the purpose of these items. A hairbrush takes a head of hair and brushes it into a masterpiece. Ice cream scoops are used to sink into a big pile of ice cream and scoop it into a bowl for the enjoyment of our tummies. Cameras capture all the memorable moments of life for us to keep.

When we look at the world around us, it's easy to point out the purpose of the things we see. But what can be a little more difficult to figure out, oftentimes, is our purpose. A camera takes pictures— but what is your purpose and mine? Why were we created? What role do we play?

Whenever we tackle questions like these, the best place we can go for answers is the Bible. The Bible is God's roadmap for our lives. It tells the story of Jesus, and it is the foundation we walk on in life.

As we search through the Bible, there is one common theme that stands out when we talk about our purpose: we were created to make a difference. You were created to make a difference for God's Kingdom. The Bible calls you and me the salt of the earth, the light of the world, and even a masterpiece—created to do good things for God that He planned long ago.

You see, these statements from the Bible are true, and they shape our identity.

Maybe in your life, people have called you mean names or said you weren't smart. Maybe you've felt like you didn't have a role to play in God's story. But those statements simply aren't true. God has a purpose specifically for you. In a world that lacks the flavors and goodness of Heaven, you are salt. You are joy when there is none, kindness when it seems lost. You are the tasty saltshaker of Heaven in a world that desperately needs the flavors Jesus brought.

Not only that, but in a dark world, you are light—shining and pointing people to the love and hope that Jesus offers. God created you to do good things and to be His child. As you and I discover who He is and allow that to shape who we are, good things flow out of us like a river. We can be helpful, we can serve, we can be kind, and we can live like Jesus. In the moments when we struggle or aren't our nicest, God shows us how to grow. If we let Him, He can make changes in our hearts so we can be the difference-makers He created us to be.

If you ever wonder, Why am I here? just look to the Bible, and the answer becomes clear.

You were created to shine. You were made to do good—even in moments when you feel misunderstood. Your purpose is obvious, and your mission is set. You are here to make a difference. Don't you ever forget.

Daily Declaration:

I am God's daughter, a daughter of the King. I was created to make a difference.

Talking to God Together:

God, thank You for creating me and giving me a purpose. I thank You for who You made me to be, and the way You designed me is wonderful. Give me the courage to make a difference in this world for You.

Make a Memory Together:

Make a difference. Before your next lesson, your challenge is to make a difference together. Maybe that means cleaning the house, serving your mom, helping a neighbor, or cooking for a friend. Make a difference together!

"But you are not like that, for you are a chosen people. You are royal priests, a holy nation, God's very own possession. As a result, you can show others the goodness of God, for he called you out of the darkness into his wonderful light."
1 Peter 2:9, NLT

Lesson 14:

Coronation Day

Today is Coronation Day!

Today is going to be a little different from any other day we've had so far. Why? Because it's Coronation Day! What does that mean? Well, it's the special day we hold a ceremony to crown God's daughters as princesses in the Kingdom of Heaven.

When God thinks of you, He calls you the head and not the tail. He says you are above and not beneath. He even goes so far as to say that you are royalty. Every single person who has accepted Jesus Christ as their Lord and Savior is adopted into God's royal family. His sons are princes, and every one of His daughters is a princess—created to show God's goodness and shine His light into the darkness around us.

Here's how today will work:

- Prepare the Room: Choose a room in your house and create a special pathway for the princess to walk down. You can use toys, flowers, or flower petals to mark the path—it's up to you!
- Dress the Princess: The princess-to-be will put on her favorite dress, outfit, or dress-up attire. She'll also find or create something that can serve as her crown.
- Set the Scene: Play some royal music to make the moment extra special.

- The Coronation: Dads, you'll need to find something to use as a "sword" for the crowning ceremony.
- When everything is ready, it's time for the royal declaration.

Dad's Script:

"Today, I, (Dad's Name), declare that (Daughter's Name) is royalty in the Kingdom of God. You are strong, brave, beautiful, and created to make a difference in this world. You are God's chosen person, a royal priest, and part of a holy nation. You are God's special possession. You radiate the goodness of God and shine the light of Jesus everywhere you go. The Holy Spirit has filled you with power, and you will live all the days of your life as royalty in the Kingdom of God. I dub thee Princess (Daughter's Name)."

Make a Memory Together:

After the coronation, finish the royal day with a tea party! Enjoy some snacks together and celebrate your new princess(es).

"Each time he said, 'My grace is all you need. My power works best in weakness.' So now I am glad to boast about my weakness, so that the power of Christ can work through me."

2 Corinthians 12:9, NLT

I Am Not Perfect, and That's Perfectly Okay

Have you ever made a really big mess? I'm not talking about a tiny spill of water or leaving a stuffed animal on the ground. I mean the kind of mess that takes days to clean up—and maybe even requires a call to the professionals.

One time, I dropped a giant-sized ketchup bottle from the top shelf of the refrigerator. It wasn't a glass bottle, but when it hit the floor, it exploded like a ketchup bomb. Suddenly, there was more ketchup than I'd ever seen in my life, covering everything. It was such an epic mess that I didn't know if I'd ever be able to clean it up.

I wish I could say that was the last mess I ever made, but the truth is, I've made more messes than I can count.

Maybe you're the kind of person who feels like losing, making mistakes, or getting into trouble is your greatest fear. Some of my loved ones really struggle with this, and honestly, I struggle with it sometimes too. There are moments when making a mistake feels like the end of the world.

In the verse we started the day with, the Apostle Paul talks about his own weaknesses. We don't know exactly what his weakness was, but we do know Paul wasn't perfect. His body wasn't 100% healthy, his attitude probably wasn't always spot-on, and I bet even Paul—the guy who wrote nearly half the New Testament—had moments when he needed to ask God for forgiveness, grace, and mercy.

Paul reminds us that God's grace—His kindness and love for us even when we don't deserve it—is all we need. God wants us to take our weaknesses, mistakes, and mess-ups and hand them over to Him.

If you struggle with math, for example, you can tell God, "I'm struggling with this," and He can work through that imperfection. When we are weak, Jesus is strong. We were never meant to be perfect—because Jesus was always supposed to be perfect for us.

He is our source, and He is our leader. Anytime you feel afraid to make a mistake, you can take what Paul learned and speak it over yourself:

"God's grace is all I need. His power works best when I am weak. I can be honest and celebrate my imperfections because Jesus is always strong."

Daily Declaration:

I am God's daughter, a daughter of the King. I am not perfect, and that's perfectly okay. Jesus is my source and my strength.

Talking to God Together:

Jesus, thank You for giving me life. I pray that any fear of making mistakes or messing up would be replaced by a desire to see Your strength made perfect in my weakness. Help me not to focus on performing or being perfect, but to live in Your kindness.

Make a Memory Together:

Make a mess together. That's right—you read that correctly! Do some finger painting, play in the grass, bake cookies and get flour all over the counter, or maybe even take a bottle of Coca-Cola, add some Mentos, and watch it explode outside your house. Create a memory together that's just a little bit messy!

"For God has not given us a spirit of fear and timidity, but of power, love, and self discipline."
2 Timothy 1:7, NLT

Lesson 16:

I am Strong and Able

Have you ever heard someone say, "You do something like a girl!"? Growing up, people around me filled in that something with all kinds of actions. "You throw like a girl," or "You hit like a girl," or "You run like a girl."

I have four daughters. Each one is different, yet each is incredibly talented in so many ways. What I've discovered is that there's almost no action out there that one of the girls in my life isn't great at.

If you say, "You drive like a girl," then you haven't met my wife—one of the best drivers I know. If you say, "You shoot like a girl," then you've never seen my oldest daughter beat all the boys at basketball. And if you say,

"You punch like a girl," then you've never been punched by my daughter, who is one of the strongest young humans I've ever had the privilege of being punched by. The truth is, girls are both strong and capable. You are fully able to become the amazing young woman God created you to be.

Yes, God made males and females different. We are distinct by design, and being the young woman God created you to be—with all the gifts, unique qualities, and purpose He placed in you—is incredible. But let me be clear: girls aren't just damsels in distress, waiting for a prince to come and save them.

Sure, I love watching those fairytale movies, but each young woman God created is capable of truly amazing things. You are smart. You create. You dream. You compete. You care. You are compassionate. And don't ever believe the lie that girls aren't enough.

One of the healthiest things a daughter of the King can do is ask God to show her how wonderfully He made her. When you see yourself through God's eyes, you'll see the strength and purpose He's placed in you.

So don't back down from a challenge or walk away from an opportunity because you're a girl. You are God's girl, and being His young lady is a gift worth celebrating.

Daily Declaration:

I am God's daughter, a daughter of the King. God designed me to be a strong, capable, and beautiful young woman.

Talking to God Together:

God, thank You for the way You made me. I ask that each day I would discover more of what it means to be Your daughter, created in Your image. Show me how to be a woman after Your heart.

Make a Memory Together:

Today's challenge is to make a list! Write down all the things you're really good at. Don't focus on the negative today—celebrate your strengths and talents. At the end, take a moment to thank God together for the way He created both the daughters and the dads!

"Don't copy the behavior and customs of this world, but let God transform you into a new person by changing the way you think. Then you will learn to know God's will for you, which is good and pleasing and perfect."

Romans 12:2, NLT

Lesson 17:

I am One of a Kind

Have you ever made Christmas sugar cookies before? I haven't, but I've watched my wife make them—and I'm an expert at eating them! With sugar cookie dough, you roll it out and use cookie cutters to create shapes. Candy canes, Santa hats, gingerbread men—whatever shape you want. You just press the cookie cutter into the dough, and that piece becomes the shape of the cutter.

If you use the same cutter for a large batch of cookies, you end up with a lot of cookies that all look the same.

I once heard from a mentor of mine, Dr. Brian Jenkins, that God isn't in the business of making cookie-cutter people. He shared with me that we are each unique, one-of-a-kind creations, handcrafted by a loving Father.

In Romans 12:2, the Apostle Paul teaches us not to allow ourselves to be pressed into the world's cookie-cutter mold. The "world" represents all the people, ideas, and beliefs that go against God's Word. Believe it or not, there's an enemy in our lives who wants us to make choices that lead us away from God.

When we give in to the world's way of living, we allow ourselves to be pressed into a mold that was never meant for us. We start to lose our uniqueness. We feel broken, lose our purpose, and let sadness and sin take over. Hope begins to fade.

But God has something so much better for us. He invites us to let Him mold, shape, and form the way we think. When we allow God to transform our minds, our thoughts begin to reflect His heart. He makes us brand new.

In God's hands, each of us becomes the unique and special person He created us to be. We begin to see His plans for our lives—and they're good!

So, do yourself a favor: don't let yourself be pressed into the world's cookie cutter. Cookie cutters can be overrated. Let God form you into the special and amazing daughter of the King that you are.

Daily Declaration:

I am God's daughter, a daughter of the King. I am one of a kind.

Talking to God Together:

God, I pray that each day I would celebrate the unique person You created me to be. Help me not to be shaped by the world, but to be shaped by Your Word.

Make a Memory Together:

Head to your local grocery store and grab some cookie dough or make some homemade dough from scratch. Shape each cookie a little differently—unique in size or design—and watch how they come out one of a kind. Then, enjoy them together with your favorite beverage.

"The tongue can bring death or life; those who love to talk will reap the consequences."
Proverbs 18:21, NLT

Lesson 18:
My Words Matter

There's an illustration out there that explains the power of words really well. It goes something like this: words are like toothpaste— once you squeeze all the toothpaste out, it's almost impossible to get it back into the tube. In the same way, words are almost impossible to take back once they've been spoken.

If I'm honest, this illustration is also a great reminder to brush your teeth! No cavities allowed! (Just joking—I've had my fair share of cavities in my day.) But no matter how many times a day you brush your teeth (let's aim for twice, okay?), we can all agree on one simple fact: words are powerful.

In Proverbs, the writer teaches us that words actually have the power to bring life or death. Think about that for a second. The words you and I speak carry that kind of weight. Imagine for a moment that you're talking to a plant. (You're not crazy, I promise.) Every time you say mean, negative words to the plant, it starts to wilt and die. But every time you speak kind, life-giving words, the plant stands taller, shines brighter, and grows stronger.

That's exactly what happens to the world around you based on the words you speak.

I'll never forget the day one of my friends, who always looked up to me, tried to join a sport I played with another group of friends. I didn't want him to hang out with us, so I made fun of him right in front of everyone. Those words were devastating, and to this day, I wish I could take them back. I didn't just lose a friendship—I used my words to harm someone who was supposed to be my friend.

As daughters of the King, each of us can speak life over ourselves and others. Your words matter. Use them to build others up, to show kindness, and to reflect the love of Jesus. The power of life and death is on your tongue—so how will you use it?

Daily Declaration:

I am God's daughter, a daughter of the King. My words are powerful, and I will use them to bring life to myself and others.

Talking to God Together:

God, I ask for forgiveness today for the times when I use my words to harm myself and others. I ask that you teach me how to use my words to bring life, to build up, and to show the love of Jesus.

Make a Memory Together:

Find a jar—this will be your Words of Life Jar.
Together, write down 10-20 encouraging words or phrases on slips of paper. Over the next few days/weeks, take one encouragement out of the jar each day, speak it over yourself, and share it with someone else. Use this as a reminder to speak life into your own heart and the hearts of others!

Just for Dads: Choose Your Pain

Now the Spirit of the Lord had left Saul, and the Lord sent a tormenting spirit that filled him with depression and fear. Some of Saul's servants said to him, "A tormenting spirit from God is troubling you. Let us find a good musician to play the harp whenever the tormenting spirit troubles you. He will play soothing music, and you will soon be well again." "All right," Saul said. "Find me someone who plays well, and bring him here." One of the servants said to Saul, "One of Jesse's sons from Bethlehem is a talented harp player. Not only that—he is a brave warrior, a man of war, and has good judgment. He is also a fine-looking young man, and the Lord is with him." So Saul sent messengers to Jesse to say, "Send me your son David, the shepherd." Jesse responded by sending David to Saul, along with a young goat, a donkey loaded with bread, and a wineskin full of wine. So David went to Saul and began serving him. Saul loved David very much, and David became his armor bearer. Then Saul sent word to Jesse asking, "Please let David remain in my service, for I am very pleased with him." And whenever the tormenting spirit from God troubled Saul, David would play the harp. Then Saul would feel better, and the tormenting spirit would go away. (1 Samuel 16:14-23, NLT)

This passage of Scripture has always been interesting to me. The people of Israel ask for a king, and God gives them Saul. He is anointed king, and God is with him.

But not too long into the story, Saul starts to act a little different from the young man God originally chose. Pride creeps in, and he disobeys God. Because of this, God removes His blessing and the Holy Spirit from Saul, and what follows is pretty dark for him.

In this passage, God allows a tormenting spirit to enter Saul's life. You would think this disturbance would cause Saul to cry out to God, surrender, repent—something. But instead, he settles for a talented musician to come and play music that would soothe him and bring temporary relief.

When in all honesty, Saul didn't need soothing—he needed deliverance, healing, and surrender to God.

As much as I'd like to judge Saul for this moment in his life, I can't without being a hypocrite.

I've found that no matter what, life will always bring pain that we have to face.

A book that has meant a lot to me in my walk with Jesus is called *The Genesis Process* by Michael Dye. In it, I was introduced to a concept called the double bind—where, on both sides of a decision, you find pain.

It's like no matter what choice you make, there will be some level of pain attached to it. The big question that comes from a double bind is:

"What pain are you willing to live with?"

Saul found himself in a situation where there was pain no matter what he did.

He could have chosen to repent, surrender, and cry out to God, but that would have meant facing the pain of letting his pride die. So instead, he chose momentary relief.

He chose to mask the pain rather than deal with it—and in doing so, he allowed depression and fear to keep returning over and over again.

As dads and as followers of Jesus, we will always be faced with this same predicament:

Which pain are you willing to live with?

The pain of surrender and honesty?

Or the pain that your brokenness is already causing you?

I've done my fair share of covering up, masking, and seeking momentary relief.

But today, I challenge you to examine your life and start stepping into the pain that brings healing, deliverance, and true freedom.

Run into the arms of a loving God—a God who is always ready to forgive and restore.

"Confess your sins to each other and pray for each other so that you may be healed. The earnest prayer of a righteous person has great power and produces wonderful results."
James 5:16, NLT

Lesson 19:
I am Honest, Even When it Hurts

Have you ever told a lie before? I remember one of the first times I ever lied. I was very young, and there was a show my parents didn't allow me to watch. One night, while they were on a date, my older sister was babysitting me. While she was upstairs, I turned the channel to that show I wasn't supposed to watch.

When my parents got home, they asked me if I had watched the show. How did they even know? Parents seem to know everything sometimes! Instead of being honest, I lied. What I didn't realize was that the TV had a feature that showed a list of all the things you'd watched. My parents checked it, and BAM—I got caught in a lie.

Maybe you can relate to my story about telling a lie. Lies are tricky because they often make us think we're protecting ourselves. But in the end, they only bring harm—to us and to others.

Whether you've told a lie or tried to keep a secret hidden, God has a better way. When we sin, there's always an opportunity to tell the truth—to God, to trusted adults, and to friends who can help us and lead us back to Jesus.

Sometimes it's really hard to tell the truth because we're afraid of getting in trouble. But as daughters of the King, we are called to be honest—even when it hurts. We don't run away from pain or try to hide. Instead, we tell the truth and trust that God is always faithful to forgive us and bring us back to His heart.

I love how James puts it when he tells us to confess our sins to each other so we can be healed. When we're honest about our sin—with God and with others—we receive forgiveness and healing.

Don't run from a secret or live with a lie that only brings harm. If you're carrying something today, be honest. God has so much more for us. He wants us to live as honest sons and daughters of the King.

Daily Declaration:

I am God's daughter, a daughter of the King. I will be honest, even when it's hard.

Talking to God Together:

Jesus, thank you for being a God of forgiveness, mercy, and grace. Help me not to run away when things get hard, but to be honest with you and with people I trust. I pray that in every situation, I would speak truth and rely on you completely.

Make a Memory Together:

Tonight's activity is called We Listen and We Don't Judge. Each person, including Dad, will have a chance to share their heart while everyone else listens. Share whatever is on your mind and end the moment with a big hug!

"Then, after doing all those things, I will pour out my Spirit upon all people. Your sons and daughters will prophesy. Your old men will dream dreams, and your young men will see visions."
Joel 2:28, NLT

Lesson 20:

I am Prophetic

Have you ever heard God speak to you before? Wouldn't that be the coolest thing ever? Maybe He'd have a booming voice coming from the clouds. What would it feel like to hear God speak? In the Old Testament, God spoke directly to people. He had a relationship with His people, and some even heard His voice.

There were these individuals called prophets—people God would speak to, who would then deliver His message to others.

Sometimes the message was a warning or correction. Other times, it was a word of encouragement. Many prophets even spoke about the coming of Jesus, hundreds of years before it ever happened. God used these prophets in incredible ways.

When Jesus came, He was fully God and fully man, and He spoke to people directly. He had relationships with them. After His death and resurrection, He sent the Holy Spirit to empower His followers to live like Him and to be in a close, personal relationship with Him. This relationship is amazing! Because of the Holy Spirit, the personal presence of Jesus lives inside of you.

Did you know that the Holy Spirit speaks God's plans, words, and wonders to you? Yes, that's right—He talks to you. Every time you open the Bible, the Holy Spirit speaks to you. The Bible is the number one-way God communicates with us. But He also speaks in other ways—through dreams, visions, guidance, a deep sense of knowing what He's saying, and sometimes even in what people describe as a still, small voice.

God still speaks to you, and He desires to speak through you. Being prophetic simply means that every daughter of the King can hear from God and share His plans, His love, and His words with those around them. Maybe the Holy Spirit will show you that someone is hurting, and you'll say something that brightens their day. Or perhaps He'll lead you to pray for a friend, offer advice, or share wisdom with someone. There might even be times when a creative idea or solution just pops into your mind—it's the Holy Spirit speaking!

You are prophetic. You can speak the love and wonders of God to everyone you meet. Learn to listen—it's a lifelong journey. Start each day by saying, "I am listening, Holy Spirit. Speak to me today."

Daily Declaration:

I am God's daughter, a daughter of the King. I am prophetic, and God speaks to me.

Talking to God Together:

Holy Spirit, I ask that You teach me to listen today. Help me to hear Your voice through Your Word and in all the ways You choose to speak to me. I love You, and I want to share Your heart with those around me.

Make a Memory Together:

Put on some worship music, spend time quietly listening for God to speak and take turns sharing what you believe God is speaking to your family. Maybe it's a Bible verse or an encouraging word for someone. Let God speak, listen, and then share what 's on your heart.

> **Just for Dads: Work in Progress**

"And I am certain that God, who began the good work within you, will continue his work until it is finally finished on the day when Christ Jesus returns." (Philippians 1:6, NLT)

Have you ever had an obstacle in your life that made you think, "Man, I could do anything if _____ wasn't in the way!"

I remember struggling with a sin in my life and thinking, "If it weren't for this one sin, I'd be just like Jesus." I truly believed that if I could just get rid of this one thing, I would be the most faithful and holy follower of Jesus. Looking back, that was a pretty dumb thought.

I was finally able to be honest about that sin and begin the process of healing and recovery. But here's what surprised me—the moment that sin was removed, I realized just how many other issues were still in my life. Instead of feeling closer to Jesus, I felt farther from Him than ever before.

Through this journey, I've come to understand something profound: I am not good. But Jesus? Jesus wasn't just good—He was perfect for me.

A counselor once shared a simple but powerful saying with me, one I now speak over myself often: "I am in Jesus, and Jesus is in me." This truth is deeply rooted in John 15, where Jesus teaches that He is the true vine and we are the branches. He is our source of true, abundant life. In Him, we bear fruit, and through the work of the Holy Spirit, we are shaped to look and live more like Jesus.

I love how John 15:5 says, "For apart from me, you can do nothing." If Jesus is our source of everything, where does that leave us? You and I are simply a work in progress. God has already begun a good work in your life, whether you believe it or not. Your story is nothing less than a miracle that God is deeply invested in.

I love how the Apostle Paul writes in Philippians 1:6 that God will continue the work He started in us. Our job isn't to strive to be good or to be better—it's to simply abide in the vine of Jesus and watch Him do His work as we follow Him faithfully.

You and I are a wonderful work in progress, and we are beloved sons of the King of kings.

Your challenge for today? Give yourself some grace. Recognize the work God has already done, and trust that He will continue it until the day He returns.

Part Three:
Just Us

A Father's Gift

○ Every good father gives gifts—but the greatest ones aren't wrapped in a box. They come from the heart.

○ Before beginning this final part of the journey, take a moment to give your daughter a Father's Gift—something that represents your promise to always love, protect, and stand by her side. This isn't about how much it costs—it's about the meaning behind it.

○ This gift will serve as a reminder that no matter where life takes her, she will always have her dad in her corner. It could be:

○ A handwritten letter filled with words of encouragement and love.

○ A small token like a bracelet, necklace, or keychain—something she can carry as a symbol of your promise.

○ A special Bible verse written just for her, declaring God's plan and your prayers over her life.

○ A spoken blessing where you look her in the eyes and tell her she is cherished, seen, and never alone.

○ Whatever you choose, let it be a gift that she can carry in her heart— a symbol of your love and the unwavering presence of her Heavenly Father.

"The Lord God placed the man in the Garden of Eden to tend and watch over it."
Genesis 2:15, NLT

Lesson 21:
Let's Talk About... Responsibility

Imagine this with me...Your dad opens a brand-new business. But this isn't just any business—it's an ice cream shop! Not just any ice cream shop, but the best one ever. Every flavor you can imagine— creamy vanilla bean, rich chocolate fudge, cotton candy swirl— endless options. And the toppings? Unlimited. Rainbow sprinkles, crushed Oreos, gooey caramel, hot fudge, gummy bears—you name it, it's there. The air smells like freshly made waffle cones, and everything about this place is straight-up amazing.

Now imagine your dad comes to you and says, "I want you to be in charge."

That's right. He's trusting you to keep the ice cream machines running, make sure the shop stays clean, and even come up with new and exciting flavors. He believes in you. He sees potential in you. And giving you this responsibility isn't just about the shop—it's about showing you that you matter.

Wouldn't that feel good? You'd feel trusted, chosen, and given a real purpose.

Did you know that from the very beginning, part of God's perfect plan for the world was to give humans responsibility? Before sin entered the picture, before anything was broken, God handed Adam and Eve work.

Genesis 2:15 says, "The Lord God took the man and put him in the Garden of Eden to work it and take care of it."

Think about that—work wasn't a punishment. It wasn't something we had to do because of sin. It was part of God's perfect design. He created an incredible world, then turned to us and said, "I'm trusting you with this. Take care of it. Work it. Love it well."

Now, let's be real—responsibility doesn't always feel exciting. Making your bed, cleaning your room, picking up after yourself? Not exactly the thrill of an all-you-can-eat ice cream bar. Sometimes it feels like a chore, especially when playing a game or watching a show seems way more fun.

But here's the thing: taking care of the little things shows God He can trust us with big things.

It's not just about making your bed—it's about learning to be disciplined. It's not just about doing your homework—it's about proving you can handle commitment. It's not just about picking up after yourself—it's about showing that you take ownership of what's been given to you.

And God sees that. He sees your faithfulness in the small things, and when the time comes, He'll open up even bigger opportunities for you.

Daily Declaration:

I am God's daughter, a daughter of the King. God has given me responsibility, and I will be faithful with what He has placed in my hands. I am trustworthy, dependable, and ready for more.

Talking to God Together:

Father, thank You for trusting me with responsibilities, big and small. Help me to see them as a blessing, not a burden. Teach me to be faithful in the little things so that I can grow into the person You've created me to be.

Make a Memory Together:

As a family, pick one small responsibility that everyone will commit to this week—maybe it's keeping a space clean, completing a task without being reminded, or taking care of something with excellence. Write it down somewhere visible and encourage each other throughout the week. At the end of the week, celebrate what you've accomplished and talk about how responsibility has helped you grow.

"Bring all the tithes into the storehouse so there will be enough food in my Temple. If you do," says the Lord of Heaven's Armies, *"I will open the windows of heaven for you. I will pour out a blessing so great you won't have enough room to take it in! Try it! Put me to the test!"*

Malachi 3:10, NLT

Lesson 22:
Let's Talk About... Money

Let's Play a Game:

Where Did It Come From?
Where does milk come from?
What is paper made out of?
How do we get cheeseburgers?
Where does honey come from?
Where do bab...(nevermind).
Now, where does money come from?

Some might say ATMs, banks, or working hard at a job. Maybe for you, money just mysteriously shows up in your wallet (lucky you!). But here's the real truth—every bit of money we have is a blessing from God.

No matter how much or how little we have, we believe that God provides, God cares for us, and God is always faithful.

Imagine for a moment that you have $100. Instead of thinking about it as your money to spend at Target on fruit snacks and cute notebooks, think about it as God's money that He has blessed you with.

If that money was God's, would you spend every last dollar on juice boxes and gummy bears? Or would you try to be a good caretaker of what He's given you?

Let's talk about how a wise daughter of the King leads well with her money.

Step 1: Give – Honor God First (10%)

Before anything else, we give 10% back to God—this is called the tithe.

Tithing teaches us obedience and trust—it reminds us that everything we have belongs to God anyway. When we put God first in our money, we allow Him to lead our finances instead of our own desires.

Step 2: Save – Be Prepared (30%)

Spending everything you have as soon as you get it? Not a great idea. Trust me, I've been there, and it's not fun.

Saving teaches patience, responsibility, and wisdom. It helps us be prepared for the future—whether it's for something we need, something unexpected, or even something bigger down the road.

Step 3: Live – Spend Wisely & Give Generously (60%)

Once we've given and saved, the rest of our money is for us to use wisely. That could mean:

✓ Buying something you need or want.

✓ Blessing someone else (maybe treating a friend or giving to missions).

✓ Investing it—learning how to grow your money instead of just spending it.

✓ Having some fun (yes, fun is allowed!).

One simple rule to follow is the 10-30-60 Rule:

- 10% to God.
- 30% saved.
- 60% to spend wisely.

If you followed this every time you got money, you'd build great habits that would help you honor God, be wise with what He's given you, and enjoy life without wasting it.

Did You Know?

The average kid accumulates about $20,000 by the time they turn 18 (allowances, gifts, jobs, etc.). If you followed the 10-30-60 Rule, you'd have saved over $6,000 by then! That's a lot of money that could be used for something meaningful, college, starting a business, blessing others, or preparing for what's next in life.

Life is expensive, but when we learn to honor God with what He gives us, we become wise leaders who don't just spend money—we steward it well.

Daily Declaration:

I am God's daughter, a daughter of the King. I will be faithful with what God gives me. I will honor Him first, save wisely, and lead well with the blessings in my hands.

Talking to God Together:

Father, thank You for providing for me. I know that everything I have comes from You. Help me to be wise, to put You first, and to use what I have for good. Teach me how to give, save, and spend in a way that honors You. Amen.

Make a Memory Together:

Find a jar, envelope, or small box and label it "God's Blessings." Together, create three sections inside: Give, Save, Live (you can use paper dividers or envelopes). The next time your daughter receives money, practice the 10-30-60 rule and physically divide it up. Make it fun—talk about how each part of the money has a purpose and how she can use it to honor God and lead well.

"Understand, therefore, that the Lord your God is indeed God. He is the faithful God who keeps his covenant for a thousand generations and lavishes his unfailing love on those who love him and obey his commands."
Deuteronomy 7:9, NLT

Lesson 23:
Let's Talk About…
Our family

Who Do You Look Like?

Have you ever been told, "Wow, you look just like your mom!" or "You have your dad's eyes!"? Maybe you've even been compared to a grandparent or an aunt. But what if you've never met the people you get your beautiful features from?

No matter what your story looks like, the truth is that who you are has been passed down from someone.

It's why your eyes are so wonderful, why your skin is that amazing color, and why your nose and ears are just perfect. And just like we inherit our looks, we can also inherit other things—like talents, habits, and even the way we handle emotions.

When I first wanted to learn more about the Bible, I started right at the beginning—Genesis! And pretty quickly, I noticed something super interesting.

There was this guy named Abraham, and one day, he got really scared. So, he asked his wife to pretend to be his sister so he wouldn't get in trouble. Now, I don't think my wife would ever go along with something like that. She'd look at me and say, "No way! That's just weird!"

But here's where it gets even stranger—Abraham's son, Isaac, ended up in the exact same situation and told the exact same lie! And then Isaac's son, Jacob? His whole name literally meant "trickster", and he spent his whole life playing tricks and telling lies.

I may not be a detective, but I can see a pattern here!

The Bible shows us that families don't just pass down physical features—they pass down habits, both good and bad. Maybe your family has a history of being kind and generous. Or maybe there are struggles that have been passed down, like fear, anger, or dishonesty.

The truth is, no family is perfect. Every family has brokenness because people aren't perfect.

But the incredible news? God can take what is broken and make it brand new. You will never find a perfect family, but you will find a perfect God who redeems, restores, and brings new life.

As your dad, my promise to you is this: The brokenness in our family will not stay broken when we surrender it to Jesus. He is the God who turns bad stories into beautiful ones, and I believe He will write a new and better future for us.

Make a Memory Together:

Grab a pen and look at the Patterns of Blessing chart below. Together, circle all the blessings you see in our family. What good things has God passed down to us? Let's celebrate the legacy of blessings He has given us!

Patterns of Blessing:

- Adventuresome
- Patient
- Loyal
- Musical or Athletic
- Generous
- Productive
- Compassionate
- Hospitable

- Honest
- Creative
- Self-Controlled
- Sense of Humor
- Christian
- Good Cook

After you've circled the blessings, take a moment to thank God for them. Then, ask Him to help us keep growing in these areas and to break any unhealthy patterns.

Daily Declaration:

I am God's daughter, a daughter of the King. God has given my family good gifts, and He can fix what is broken. I will follow Him and help make our story full of love and faith.

Talking to God Together:

God, thank You for the blessings You have passed down to our family. We know that no family is perfect, but we also know You are a God who makes all things new. Help us grow in the good things You have given us, and help us trust You to heal and change the broken things. We surrender our family to You. In Jesus 'name, Amen.

"But when you are praying, first forgive anyone you are holding a grudge against, so that your Father in heaven will forgive your sins, too."
Mark 11:25, NLT

Lesson 24:
Let's Talk About... Forgiveness

To start off today, I want you to make a fist. Now take that fist and clench it as tightly as you can. Squeeze it hard, feeling your fingers start to hurt a little bit, and hold that for 10 seconds. Now let it go and relax your hand slowly. That feeling of letting go is pretty awesome after squeezing so hard, right?

If you've ever held something heavy or touched something really hot, you know how uncomfortable it can be. The relief that comes when you drop the heavy thing or let go of the hot item is amazing.

In life, there will be moments when you experience something heavy—not in your hands, but in your heart. Maybe a friend treated you badly, someone called you a mean name, or a person you trust let you down. It hurts. It's okay to feel sad, cry, or even get angry when life isn't fair.

But Jesus showed us something powerful: we can choose to forgive with His help.

On the day Jesus died, people yelled at Him, hurt Him, and treated Him terribly. Instead of trying to get back at them, Jesus looked up to His Father and said, "Forgive them, for they don't know what they are doing."

Can you imagine forgiving people who treated you so badly? That's what Jesus did.

As Daughters of the King, we choose to forgive and let go of the heavy burden of holding onto hurt. Forgiveness doesn't mean what someone did is okay. It means you give your hurt to God, let

Him heal your heart, and trust Him to take care of the person who hurt you.

Forgiveness is choosing love even when someone doesn't deserve it. Don't hold onto something heavy when you can give it to Jesus.

Daily Declaration:

I am God's daughter, a daughter of the King. I choose to forgive because Jesus forgave me. I let go of hurt and trust God to heal my heart.

Talk to God Together:

Jesus, sometimes my heart feels heavy when people hurt me. Thank You for showing me how to forgive, just like You did on the cross. Help me to let go and give my hurt to You. Heal my heart and help me to love like You do. Amen.

Make a Memory Together:

Find something around your house that's just heavy enough— something that when your dad picks it up, he can really feel it. Now, you do the same! Pick something that's heavy, but not too heavy for you.
Now it's game time! Who can last the longest?
Hold your item above your head with one hand and don't let go. First one to drop it loses!
And here's the fun part... the loser has to clean up the house before bed!
Good luck! May the strongest (or most determined) win!

But the Lord said to Samuel, "Don't judge by his appearance or height, for I have rejected him. The Lord doesn't see things the way you see them. People judge by outward appearance, but the Lord looks at the heart."
1 Samuel 16:7, NLT

Lesson 25:
Let's Talk About...
Beauty

Have I ever told you that you are beautiful? If I don't say it enough, I apologize. The truth is, you are beautiful in every way.

In our world, beauty is often measured by appearance—hair, clothes, makeup, or the way someone looks on the outside. TV shows, magazines, and social media try to define beauty in a certain way. But the Bible has something very different to say about beauty.

 Proverbs 31:30
"Charm is deceptive, and beauty does not last; but a woman who fears the Lord will be greatly praised."

 1 Peter 3:3-4
"Don't be concerned about the outward beauty of fancy hairstyles, expensive jewelry, or beautiful clothes. You should clothe yourselves instead with the beauty that comes from within, the unfading beauty of a gentle and quiet spirit, which is so precious to God."

Now, does this mean you can't curl your hair, wear your favorite necklace, or put on your best dress? Of course not! But it does mean that true beauty goes far beyond all of these things.

True beauty comes from who you are inside—from loving God and letting the Holy Spirit transform your heart, mind, and emotions.

You are a daughter of the King, and your beauty shines from the inside out.

In 1 Samuel, God tells the prophet Samuel to anoint a new king over Israel. Samuel goes to a town called Bethlehem and is ready to choose one of Jesse's sons. Some of Jesse's older sons looked impressive—probably strong, tall, and handsome. But God tells Samuel:

 Samuel 16:7

"People judge by outward appearance, but the Lord looks at the heart."

God sees true beauty in the heart. That means your kindness, love, faith, and character are what make you truly beautiful.

My daughter, you are beautiful in every single way. When you walk into the room, you take my breath away. From the top of your head to the bottom of your toes, you are perfect, no matter your clothes. But more important than what's on the outside is the beautiful heart God has placed inside of you. Let your inner beauty shine and know that you are one of a kind—a daughter of the King, beautiful in every single way.

Daily Declaration:

I am God's daughter, a daughter of the King. My beauty comes from within, not just from the outside. I will shine with kindness, love, and joy because I am wonderfully made by God.

Talk to God Together:

Jesus, thank You for making me beautiful inside and out. Sometimes, I feel pressure to look a certain way, but You remind me that true beauty comes from my heart. Help me to focus on what really matters—loving You and loving others. Let my heart shine with Your love, joy, and kindness. Amen.

Make a Memory Together:

Tonight, we're flipping beauty standards on their head with a Dad-Daughter Makeover!

Daughters, it's your turn to be the stylist! Grab some hair ties, clips, a brush, and even some (washable) makeup. Give Dad the best makeover ever—maybe some fancy hair, a stylish outfit, or even some hilarious accessories!

But there's a catch...

After Dad's transformation, he gets to return the favor! That's right—Dad gets to do your makeover too. (But don't worry, no crazy colors unless you say so!)

Just for Dads: Hidden No More

"How can a young person stay pure? By obeying your word. I have tried hard to find you—don't let me wander from your commands. I have hidden your word in my heart, that I might not sin against you." (Psalms 119:9-11, NLT)

One area of life I am praying more men have the courage to be open and vulnerable about is the struggle with lust and everything that comes with it. For me, there are specific moments from my childhood I wish had gone differently.

Whether it was the moment something inappropriate happened to me, the day I watched a scene in a movie I shouldn't have, or the time a friend on the school bus showed me something that made me more curious than I should have been—those moments left a mark on my life. What if they had never happened? Maybe parts of my story would have turned out differently.

Nevertheless, I battled addiction in the area of inappropriate online activity for many years. I became a husband, a father, and even a pastor without addressing this dark part of my life. This destructive, shameful, secret part of me nearly destroyed everything.

I remember a dream I had once. I was preaching outside to a large crowd when snakes began slithering through the people. My protective instincts kicked in, and I leapt high over the crowd, trying to grab something to save them. I spotted a weed whacker nearby, but as I reached for it, I saw a tiny snake with four legs standing just a few feet away. I'm terrified of snakes, and for some reason, this little one shook me to my core. I jumped higher than a two-story building to escape, but no matter how high I went, the snake jumped just as high. It was always right there beside me. I woke up sweating and breathing heavily, as if I had just finished running for my life. I went into another room, fell on my face, and cried out to God, asking Him what the dream meant.

I don't often hear from God through dreams, but I knew this was more than just a bad dream. In a still, small voice, God spoke to me:

"Freddie, there is something you have allowed in your life, and no matter how high I desire to take you, unless you deal with it, it will always go with you."

I knew exactly what He was talking about. But at that moment, I wasn't ready to face it head-on. It wasn't until a later season—by the grace of God—that I was able to confess everything and find true freedom.

I'm writing this today as someone who can testify that God heals, restores, and helps us walk in recovery and freedom from pornography and sexual addiction. As dads, grandpas, uncles, and father figures, I feel a deep burden for us to be more open about this struggle.

In a world flooded with oversexualized content and instant access to temptation, it's time for more men to step into healthy healing communities—places of honesty and freedom that crush shame by offering grace. It's time we face the pain and become examples to our daughters of what a man of God looks like. Not perfect—but honest, accountable, and willing to go on a journey of healing.

If you find yourself in this fight today, I want you to know that I'm with you. I pray you find the courage to face this head-on and invite the right people into your battle.

Here are a few resources and pieces of advice that have made a huge impact on my life:

1. Tell the right people & seek help.

I didn't experience true healing until I was fully honest with my wife, my leaders, and the trusted people in my life. I entered a program where my counselors led me through The Genesis Process by Michael Dye. This journey, paired with deep heart and brain work, helped me realize that porn wasn't even the real issue. I had been suppressing, avoiding, and running from pain—trying to cope with a life I had led myself into. That meant I was no match for this battle on my own.

I know Pure Desire Ministries has helped many people find

freedom and healing, and they also use The Genesis Process. Get the help you need—no matter what it takes.

2. Get into a group.

Walking into a Celebrate Recovery meeting for the first time was one of the hardest things I've ever done. But when the worship started playing, I broke down in tears. I was surrounded by people on the same journey—healing from hurts, habits, and hang-ups.

From there, I was able to build a team of guys I could turn to with questions, temptations, and struggles—men who speak into my life, challenge me, and always have an ear to listen.

3. Remove whatever needs to be removed.

This might sound extreme, but if there's a device or anything in your life that causes you to stumble, remove it—it's not worth it.

I've put up guardrails that have helped me stay free and guard against potential temptations that arise. For example:

- On my iPhone, I was able to get my phone set up with restrictions so that I only have access to texting, calling, and emails. I don't have an internet browser, and links don't open for me. This has made my phone a safe place and given me so much peace.
- I have *Covenant Eyes* on my work laptop, with my boss as my accountability partner.
- I've made a promise not to watch TV when I'm alone. It might sound weird or excessive, but these practices have helped me tremendously. I'm able to live more openly and honestly—with less fear.

I am a dad to four daughters, and my greatest desire is to be a protector and to live in a way that honors God, my wife, and my family. I haven't always done that. But I'm grateful for God's grace and mercy—for another chance to live for Him and walk in freedom.

*"Seek the Kingdom of God above
all else, and live righteously, and he
will give you everything you need."*
Matthew 6:33, NLT

Lesson 26:
Let's Talk About...Boys
(Part 1 - Crushes)

Get ready, because today we're going to talk about something kinda crazy... having a crush!

Have you ever watched a movie where a girl sees a guy, and suddenly they're getting married? I can think of one where the boy and the girl finish each other's... sandwiches—and after just one day, they decide they're going to get married. Aye!

Did you know that liking a boy is actually part of God's design for you as Daughters of the King? It may sound a little weird, but in the very beginning, when God created Adam, He said it wasn't good for Adam to be alone. So, God made Eve from Adam's rib. And fun fact— if you ever hear a boy say he's better than girls, you can jokingly remind him that boys were made from dirt, but girls were made from a rib! I'd say prime rib is way better than dirt—so girls definitely win that one!

When Adam saw Eve, he was probably like, "Whoa! Sweet rainbow unicorns, she is awesome!" (Okay, maybe not exactly like that, but you get the idea.) Feelings, crushes, and liking boys are actually a part of the way God designed us.

But here's the big thing: What we do with those feelings is really important. The Bible tells us to guard our hearts because our feelings help shape the path we walk. As we grow, we want to learn how to handle our feelings wisely. One of the best things we can do is talk to our parents or a trusted adult about what we're feeling.

Yeah, it might feel a little weird (and maybe even make your face turn red!) to tell your parents about a crush, but it's super important.

When we share what's on our hearts, we can get good advice, learn how to treat others kindly, and grow strong friendships. And most importantly, we want to keep God first. He teaches us about our feelings, guides us in His perfect plan, and helps us grow as His daughters.

So, no matter what—put God first, and He will show you how to navigate friendships, feelings, and life in the best way possible!

Daily Declaration:

I am God's daughter, a daughter of the King. My worth comes from God, not from who likes me. I will guard my heart, seek wisdom, and put God first.

Talk to God Together:

Jesus, thank You for making me with feelings and emotions. Help me guard my heart, be wise, and always put You first. Remind me that I am fully loved by You. Amen.

Make a Memory Together:

Tonight is Karaoke Night! Pick your favorite song and get ready to rock the stage! Whether it's a solo, duet, or full-family performance, everyone has to join in—no excuses! Grab a microphone (or a hairbrush), turn up the music, and let the fun begin!

"Guard your heart above all else, for it determines the course of your life."
Proverbs 4:23, NLT

Lesson 27:
Let's Talk About…Boys (Part 2 - Dating)

When I was in elementary school, there was a little girl who thought I was pretty awesome. She had a HUGE crush on me. One day, she even sent her friends over to tackle me in the sandbox and hold me down so she could swoop in and give me a kiss—YUCK! Needless to say, she really wanted me to be her boyfriend.

These days, I hear more and more young kids saying they have a boyfriend or girlfriend, and honestly? That's kinda weird to me. You see, dating isn't actually something you'll find in the Bible. Back in Bible times, things worked very differently. But what is in the Bible is God's design—a man and a woman coming together as husband and wife to honor God together. That means the feelings we have toward the opposite gender are part of God's plan for marriage one day.

Now, I have a big question for you, Daughter of the King…

Are you ready to get married right now? Are you ready to leave your parents, get a job, pay for all your own stuff, make your own dinner, buy a house, and take care of yourself with no help at all?

Even if you say yes, I have a feeling you might be fibbing just a little bit.

Maybe your friends at school or people on TV talk about dating, and it seems cool or exciting. But right now, at this time in your life, you don't need to worry about dating. One rule I always like to share is this: Whenever your mom and dad say it's okay to date, that's when you can start. Until then, it's not something you need to focus on.

The Bible teaches us to guard our hearts (Proverbs 4:23). How do we do that? By carefully watching what we think about, listen to, watch, and say. As Daughters of the King, we guard our hearts by remembering who we belong to—God! You are His girl, and your focus should be on growing in your faith, learning, loving those around you, and becoming the young woman He created you to be.

A time will come—maybe when you're 47 (just kidding!)—when you're ready to think about dating. Until then, honor God and honor your parents. If a boy asks you to be his girlfriend, you can smile, say no, and keep being the incredible Daughter of the King that God made you to be.

Daily Declaration:

I am God's daughter, a daughter of the King. My heart belongs to God, and I will trust His timing for my life. I will focus on growing in faith, loving others, and guarding my heart with wisdom.

Talk to God Together:

Jesus, thank You for creating me with feelings and emotions. Help me to guard my heart, seek wisdom, and trust Your perfect plan for my life. Remind me that my worth is found in You, and I am fully loved just as I am. Amen.

Make a Memory Together:

Tonight, let's have some fun imagining who God is shaping you to be! Grab some paper and markers and draw a picture of what you think your life will look like when you're older—your job, family, and what you'll love doing! Write down three things you want to be known for as you grow (Kind? Brave? A leader? A worshipper?).

Share your drawings and words with your family and talk about how trusting God today helps us become the person He made us to be.

"This explains why a man leaves his father and mother and is joined to his wife, and the two are united into one."
Genesis 2:24, NLT

Lesson 28:
Let's Talk About...Boys (Part 3 - Marriage)

Imagine with me for just one moment—it's your wedding day. There are flowers everywhere, a big party later with delicious food, and of course, there will be cake! Your hair is all done up, you got to put on makeup, wear pretty shoes, and a dress that makes you feel like a princess. Or maybe you dream of a simpler wedding—just you, your family, and your closest friends, dancing the night away with the person you love, ready to spend forever being best friends.

Weddings. Marriage. All of it is a pretty amazing thing.

One day, my prayer is that you get the chance to walk down the aisle and marry someone you love. But today, daughter, I want to take a moment to encourage you and speak life into you.

Every day, you are becoming the person God designed you to be. Each new morning is a chance to walk hand in hand with the King of the whole universe. He talks with you. He loves you. That King created marriage to be a beautiful and sacred relationship between one man and one woman. From that incredible promise comes the journey of becoming a family and living for the glory of God all the days of your life.

So as you dream about maybe being married one day, I want you to think about two things: who you are becoming and what kind of person you want to find one day.

Who are you becoming?

Are you growing into a daughter of the King—someone who loves and walks with Jesus, being led by the Holy Spirit? Are you kind? Do you forgive easily? Do you protect and care for your heart, letting your inner beauty shine? Become the girl God made you to be.

What kind of person do you want to find?

Be picky—it's okay to wait for the right person! Find someone who loves Jesus and is willing to live his whole life for God. Find someone who is honest, who tells the truth, and who asks for help when he struggles. Find someone who loves you for who you are and makes you laugh until you cry.

Find someone who makes you smile and gives you butterflies in your tummy. Someone who works hard and is willing to make sacrifices for his family. Find a man who is kind to you and learns how to love you the way Jesus loves His Church.

Daughter, dream big. Ask God to walk with you. Live each day knowing He has a beautiful future planned for you.

One day, if God allows, I pray I get to walk you down the aisle. I hope I'll have enough money to help give you a beautiful wedding. I pray I get to kiss your cheek and hand you off to a young man who loves Jesus and loves you the way you deserve.

I love you, my daughter. Today and for the rest of forever.

Daily Declaration:

I am God's daughter, a daughter of the King. God loves me and has a plan for my life. I will be kind, love others, and trust Him with my future. If I get married one day, I will wait for someone who loves Jesus and treats me well!

Talk to God Together:

Dear Jesus, thank You for loving me and having a plan for my life. Help me be kind, love others, and follow You every day. If I get married one day, please bring me someone who loves You and treats me well. Until then, help me trust You and grow into who You made me to be. Thank You for my family and for always being with me. Amen.

Make a Memory Together:

"My Future Husband List"
Grab a notebook and some fun pens! Talk about the kind of person your daughter hopes to marry one day—not just what he looks like, but the kind of heart he has. Help her think of things like:
Loves Jesus
Is kind and honest Makes me laugh
Works hard and cares for others Loves me for who I am
Is my best friend
Let her add anything special to her list. When she's done, fold it up and keep it somewhere safe. Remind her that she doesn't have to worry about this now—God is writing her story, and right now, He's helping her become the amazing girl He made her to be!

Just for Dads: Restore Eden

"God blesses those who are poor and realize their need for him, for the kingdom of heaven is theirs. God blesses those who mourn, for they will be comforted. God blesses those who are humble, for they will inherit the whole earth. God blesses those who hunger and thirst for justice, for they will be satisfied. God blesses those who are merciful, for they will be shown mercy. God blesses those whose hearts are pure, for they will see God. God blesses those who work for peace, for they will be called the children of God." (Matthew 5:3-9, NLT)

For a while now, I've had this concept of Restoring Eden in my mind. What would it look like for God's original design to be restored in each of us? His original intent for our purpose, relationships, minds, bodies, sexuality, and families?

One of my favorite passages in Scripture is the Beatitudes, recorded in Matthew at the beginning of the Sermon on the Mount. This is the longest recorded message we have from Jesus. I love listening to good preaching, but if Jesus is the one preaching, you better believe I'm leaning in.

Jesus opens this life-changing sermon by teaching what it truly means to be blessed. Some translations even use the word happy. As I've studied the Beatitudes, I've come to see them as a road map—a journey that leads to true blessing, deep joy, and lasting freedom. Each blessing opens the door to the next, like a domino effect, ultimately culminating in the greatest reward: an unshakable faith that can withstand trials, persecution, and difficulty, with a heavenly reward beyond compare.

This road begins with being poor in spirit. It's a heart posture that recognizes its sin, its shortcomings, and surrenders to the lordship of Jesus. From this place of humility comes mourning—not just sorrow, but a deep awareness that the life we once held onto must be laid down. This mourning is a beautiful kind of brokenness. It's a holy grief that leads to repentance—the painful yet obedient steps of making right the pain we've caused.

Then, something shifts. Meekness begins to shape us. Pride loosens its grip. We start seeing the world through new eyes—no longer centered on me, but on the work God is doing around us. A hunger grows within us, a longing for righteousness, for God's Word, for His design. And as we are cleansed from our past, we find ourselves extending mercy, because we have received it. Our hearts change— not by force, not by white-knuckling it—but by the transformative power of a renewed spirit, mind, and soul.

This transformation is undeniable. We go from Mr. Macho to peacemaker—not weak, but strong in a new way. No longer fighting to prove ourselves, but fighting for unity, for truth, for God's kingdom to be restored.

This is the journey of Restoring Eden—of returning to the life God originally intended for us to walk in. It's not easy. It requires surrender. But it leads to the greatest joy, the truest freedom, and the most lasting reward.

"*I have told you all this so that you may have peace in me. Here on earth you will have many trials and sorrows. But take heart, because I have overcome the world.*"
John 16:33, NLT

Lesson 29:

Let's Talk About... Something Weird (Safe Sharing)

Have you ever had something happen in life that was a little hard to talk about?

When I was a kid, I went to a birthday party at a swimming pool. All my friends were great swimmers—but I wasn't. They all jumped into the pool, doing big cannonballs. Not wanting to seem lame, I jumped in after them, hoping that somehow I'd magically become a great swimmer once I hit the water.

Let's just say... that didn't happen. Instead, a lifeguard had to drag me out of the pool and rescue me because I almost drowned!

For some reason, I didn't want my parents to know about the accident. I felt embarrassed. I felt ashamed. I just wanted that memory to go away. But my friend's mom told my parents, and they were pretty freaked out. Looking back, I'm really glad they found out. Because after that, they put me in swimming lessons, and I became a strong swimmer. But if my parents hadn't known about what happened at that birthday party, I don't know if I ever would have learned.

In the Bible, Jesus promises us that we will go through hard things. That doesn't seem like a fun promise, does it? Why would He tell us that difficult things will happen? Well, because we live in a broken world, and tough times are just part of life. Weird things happen, scary things happen, unfair things happen—sometimes things that don't make sense.

And as humans, sometimes things happen in our bodies, our minds, and our lives that just feel... weird.

There may even come a time when something happens that you don't feel like sharing. But today, I want us to make a promise to each other: in our family, we share the weird things.

If something feels embarrassing to say, or weird to talk about, this is a safe place. You can always come to me and say, "I have something weird to talk about," or "I have something hard to say."

And I promise to listen. I promise to do my best to understand. I promise to always love you. And I promise to ask God to show us the best next step in whatever weird or hard thing life throws our way.

No matter what happens, we're going to get through it together!

Daily Declaration:

I am God's daughter, a daughter of the King. He cares about every part of my life. I don't have to be afraid to share the hard or weird things because I am loved and safe. No matter what happens, I will trust God, knowing He is always with me!"

Talk to God Together:

Jesus, thank You for always being with me. Sometimes life feels weird or hard, but I know I can trust You. Help me to be brave and share what's on my heart. Remind me that I am loved, safe, and never alone. Amen.

Make a Memory Together:

Get ready to embrace the weird! Your challenge today is to make some food that's a little unusual... and eat it! Try putting hot sauce on a PB&J, dipping a pickle in strawberry jam, or mixing ketchup with your mac & cheese. You could even make a crazy snack combo like bananas with ranch dressing or popcorn with mustard!

The only rule? You have to take a bite! Have fun, get creative, and enjoy the weirdness!

"See how very much our Father loves us, for He calls us His children, and that is what we are!"
1 John 3:1, NLT

Lesson 30:

Let's Dance

You did it! You have officially made it to the end of the daughters of the King journey. But the amazing thing about this journey is that finishing this book is just the beginning of all that God will do in each daughter's life and in the beautiful bond between every dad and his little girl.

Today, I want you to find a song that will be your special Father-Daughter song—one that you choose together. Put on your best out-fit, clear some space, and spend time dancing with your daughter(s).

I pray a blessing over every home, every marriage, and every family that has been part of this daughters of the King journey. You are not alone—there are courageous men and incredible daughters all over the world growing in their faith and love for one another.

Daughters, you are a daughter of the King forever. Dads, you are sons of the Most High God.

Now, let's dance.

Just for Dads: You Got This, Bro

Hey bro,

By making it this far, the only thing I can say is—wow. I am proud of you. I don't know if that means much, but man, I am cheering you on.

Being here today means you took up the challenge of being a courageous dad—choosing to lay a foundation for your daughter to walk on. Your decision to be a man, a father, a husband, and a leader who follows Jesus is going to make an impact far beyond what you can see in this life.

I don't think we talk enough about the weight of being a dad who is truly trying. The reality is, so many men fail—not because they want to, but because the heaviness of life can be overwhelming. There was a season in my life where I struggled to be present with my family because I felt like I could never provide a life my kids could be proud of. I felt insecure, almost like I wanted someone else to take that responsibility.

But brother, that is a lie.

There's a song by Sanctus Real called "Lead Me." I've played it on repeat so many times, sitting in failure, grief, and doubt, wondering if I was enough to lead my wife and kids—to be the man God was calling me to be.

If you've ever felt that way, let me remind you of the truth.

As we finish this journey together, I want to speak some life into the man you are and the dad you're becoming:

- You are strong and courageous.
- You are a mighty man of God.
- You are a man of integrity.
- You are a son of the King. He loves you and is proud of you.
- No circumstance, no sin, no past mistake can take away God's love for you.
- You are more than enough. And at the same time, you aren't enough—you need God.

But here's the good news:
God is writing a story with your life. One step at a time.
One day at a time. One miracle at a time.

You got this, bro.

www.ingramcontent.com/pod-product-compliance
Lightning Source LLC
Chambersburg PA
CBHW051313120626
46547CB00015B/2221